NICHOLE FORBES

Finding Me in Him

*one woman's journey
to discovering
her identity in Christ*

 **FriesenPress**

Suite 300 – 990 Fort Street
Victoria, BC, Canada V8V 3K2
www.friesenpress.com

ISBN
978-1-4602-5442-4 (Hardcover)
978-1-4602-5443-1 (Paperback)
978-1-4602-5444-8 (eBook)

1. Religion, Christian Life, Inspirational

Distributed to the trade by The Ingram Book Company

TABLE OF CONTENTS

Section Four 115

To
Gavin, Meghan and Zane
May you lose yourself in Jesus everyday

INTRODUCTION

I ONCE WAS LOST, BUT NOW I'M FOUND.

I'm writing the beginning at the end. I've just spent the last several months writing, revising, editing and reworking this wee book that has now found its way into your hands. And after months of writing - and years of living - this book, the one thing I know for sure is that I once was lost but now I'm found.

There are a million different ways to be lost. There's the kind of lost you get when you won't ask for directions. There's the kind of lost you get when you don't know your left from right. There's the kind of lost you get when you get on the wrong train or bus. There's the kind of lost you get when you try to follow a story that a three year old is telling. And then there's the kind of lost you get when you sleep walk through years of your life only to wake up and wonder how the heck you ended up here. That's the kind of lost I once was.

I spent years doubting myself and doubting God's presence in my life. I second-guessed every decision I made. I tried to earn my way into worthiness and righteousness but at the same time I down–played every God-given strength I had. I was a disaster of my own creation on the inside while I lived the charade of an average Christian gal on the outside. I was desperately unhappy and felt my lostness every day of my life. Although I wasn't sure of who or where I was God knew exactly where to find me.

He sought me out. He found me. He wooed me. He brought me into relationship with Him. He made me alive and opened my eyes to His purpose, His love, His life. He found me and I found myself in Him.

This book started off as a letter to my eldest son. He was feeling down and out of place in this world so I wrote him a letter to remind him of the simple truth that God knows him, created him and has a beautiful plan for his life. That letter, in part, became The Psalm 139 chapter. From there the words just kept flowing. Truth after truth about God's love for me flooded my heart and I was compelled to write them down.

Scripture verses came to mind and as I read them monumental life events and seemingly insignificant everyday happenings came to my remembrance. Each one was another example of God's unending pursuit, His unfailing love and His limitless hope for me. His daughter. The one He loves.

As I wrote I saw a pattern emerge. Every instance that the enemy planned for harm in my life God turned into an occasion to celebrate. Every rough edge of my personality became a moment for God's grace to reshape me. Every thing that could disqualify me from being a person of value God used to show His glory and His goodness. Every step of the way God has turned what the devil meant to destroy me into the very thing He needed to proclaim His love for me. Amazing!

What's more amazing is that your story is exactly the same! God loves you just as much as He loves me. He is pursuing you just as He continues to pursue me. And everything He has done, and continues to do for me, He will do for you. He is able and willing to do exceedingly, abundantly above and beyond what you could ever ask or think – because He loves you.

How magnificent!

My prayer for you, as you settle into this book, is that you lose yourself in Christ, in His goodness, His faithfulness and His love. Lose yourself and be found. In Him!

THINGS YOU SHOULD KNOW

I have been a blogger for a number of years. I write about my family, motherhood and all the craziness that comes with my Random life. When I started the blog I decided to use nicknames for my loved ones. I joke that I used them to protect the guilty and the insane but in truth, I wanted to give my kids a little deniability wiggle room. As I set out to write this book I tried to use their real names but it felt awkward and unnatural so they are, as they have ever been in print, Mr. Awesome, Dude, Crafty and Mischief and I, as always, am just Some Random Mother.

You may also come across a few words that are 'Nic-isms' such as lostness, unlovliness and IGIMs. There is no explanation for this other than, when you're the writer you get to make the rules. In my world anything can be a word when '-ness' is attached to it and an IGIM is an excellent thing to get.

An IGIM is an 'I Got it Moment' otherwise known as an epiphany, light bulb moment or revelation. It's the moment when things suddenly click into place in your mind and make sense. This whole book, in essence, is an IGIM.

Although I am a rule follower by nature, there are no rules when it comes to reading this book. There are 30 chapters so in theory you can us it as a one-chapter-a-day devotional. The chapters follow the flow of my life and learning curve but you can read these chapters out of order, back to front or play reading roulette and start reading wherever the book falls open. Although I wrote this book, it's not mine. It's yours. Read it, reference it, re-gift it, use it however you like. Get comfy with it, underline, make notes and add to it. This is as much your story as mine.

Section

One

Belonging

Preppy. Jock. Grunge. Mod. Nerd. Boho. University Casual. Bible School Modest is Hottest. Mommy Jean Fab. Yoga Pant Chic.

For a lot of years my whole life revolved around finding some group to fit in to, some club, clique, trend or sub culture that would accept me as one of their own. My teens and early twenties were spent flip-flopping through fashion trends while struggling to define my taste, my style and my identity. I was the worst chameleon ever. No one has ever stood out so much while trying so desperately to blend in. The more I tried to define myself, the more lost I felt.

My struggle with my identity wasn't just based on style trends and cultural movements. It went deeper than that, right to my very heart. I felt like I was always on the outside looking in. I felt that I was missing something, that one thing that would make all the pieces come together. I struggled with never feeling pretty enough, clever enough, interesting enough or talented enough. There was nothing special about me, nothing that would draw people to me, nothing that would make people want to know me.

I wish I could tell you that I had a grand epiphany, that I had read some book that changed my life or that I had a come-to-Jesus experience that broke through my insecurities and healed my fractured heart in one fell swoop. I wish I could but I can't. My journey to discovering my true identity has been, well, a journey. It has come in fits and starts, in quiet moments of Christ discovery and after full-scale emotional meltdowns. This has been a messy, gut-wrenching, pride-breaking, heart-mending, beautiful transformation and all the while God has been with me.

This process began at some undefined moment when I realized that the Bible is written about me. All those verses about God's love, His plans, His protection for His people are actually about me. I am His people. When He says, "You are My child. You belong to Me," He is actually talking to me. He chose me and He continues to choose me.

I'm still walking this journey of understanding to who He says I am, who I am to Him and how that shapes my life but there are fewer meltdowns and more quiet moments. Each time God whispers into my heart it is easier for me to hear Him, to recognize His voice and accept His truth. And the more I listen, the more He speaks.

And He'll speak to you, too.

Be still. Listen to the beat of your heart. Hear those words echo in your own being for He has whispered them to you, too. Every moment of every day He calls to you, "You are Mine. I choose you ... you belong to Me."

Chapter *One*

A HOLY OATH

Leviticus 20:26

And you shall be holy to Me, for I the Lord am holy, and have separated you from the peoples, that you should be Mine.

Written within the pages of Leviticus is one of the greatest love stories in history. Actually this love story starts in Exodus and continues into the book of Joshua, or maybe it starts in Genesis and is still unfolding today. Either way, it's the story of a wayward people and a loving God. It's the story of a lost child and a searching Father. It's the story of love reunited. An in the most unlikely of places, right in the middle of laws and procedures, in some of the most boring and dogmatic language imaginable, is a beautiful declaration of love.

"That you should be Mine."

God is reminding His children that in the beginning He chose them. He declared to them that everything He had done from the moment of their separation until the moment of their reconciliation and beyond was for this one purpose, that they could be His. He pulled them out of their ordinary lives and completely reshaped their destiny because of His love for them. This had been His intention all along.

God first made this commitment to His children when they were in Egypt, when they were still lowly slaves. *I will take you as My people and I will be your God. (Exodus 6:7)* This statement has the sound of marriage vows about it but it carries a weightier promise. This is a holy oath that passes through this life and into eternity. This is the moment when God claimed these people as His own, when He reclaimed them, when He redeemed them with His love. They had no status and no wealth. They had no appearance of value; they had no name and no country of their own. These people were merely existing but not truly living. Yet, God came looking for them. He saw them for who they could be. He saw that they could be His.

It took more than a declaration of love from God to woo His people. They were wary, shallow and fickle. Even though they were the ones who had wandered from Him, they still wanted proof of His love. They wanted grand gestures and overt displays and when the Father God who loved them with an endless love obliged, they wanted more.

He rescued them with a magnificent show of power. He protected them, strengthened them and provided for them. Through plagues, raging seas and fierce enemies He shielded them. With clouds of smoke and pillars of fire He guided them. With heavenly bread and supernatural provisions He fed them. He cleared a path before them, chasing armies and adversaries from their presence. Every step of the way He loved, protected and pursued His children.

It took years and years, a generation, of mighty displays but God's people finally began to understand the power, scope and possibilities of His love. They let down their guard; they relaxed into Him. They fully became His and claimed Him for their own. In the moment of their surrender to the fullness of His love they went from being ordinary to being extraordinary. In that final release of their own ideas of themselves they became what their Father always knew they could be; His own, special, set apart, a chosen people.

I had my own drawn–out courtship with God. I let Him rescue me, protect me and provide for me. I was aware of Him. I witnessed His grand gestures and subtle whispers of love to me. I knew He was pursuing me but I didn't see Him for who He really is. He was just God, always there, in the distance and I was me, stuck in my ordinary, going–nowhere life. As long as I thought I was being pursued by an ordinary God I lived an ordinary life. The moment I understood that God, the magnificent Creator of the universe, the Beginning and the End, the Everlasting, My Everything, was pursuing me everything changed.

When I realized that an extraordinary God loved me, my life became extraordinary in Him. I became His and He became mine. I fell in love with Him and that love, rather the acceptance of that love, ruined me for the ordinary. I was no longer content with living day to day, with being average. I wanted more of Him, more of His love. This amazing love pulled me out of the crowd and transformed me into the very person He always knew I could be. His own.

When the children of Israel fully accepted God's love they stopped wandering and started possessing. They no longer floundered, unsure of their identity. They walked in full confidence as children of The Most High God. They claimed all that He had given them for their own because they were His. Likewise, when I accepted the fullness of God's love I stopped existing and started living. This acceptance meant I no longer had to struggle with my identity and self-worth. I was free to claim the title of Daughter of the Most High God for my own. I was free to be who He created me to be.

This didn't come easy for me though. I always felt the need to apologize, through word or tone, for anything and everything good in my life. I could never graciously accept a compliment because I never felt worthy of the blessings or abilities I had. I chronically downplayed my role in anything that was a success because I felt I hadn't earned the right to be an asset. What I was missing was the understanding that I was capable of doing good, of being worthy of approval, simply because God created me. I didn't need to earn anything. In fact, there was no possible way for me to earn what He had already freely given. He gave me His love and He called me His own.

When we recognize God's love for what it is, a free, no-strings-attached gift from a loving Father, we too can relax into it. When we accept His love, He is then free to show us who we really are because it is in His love that we are defined, explained and purposed. There is a security and peace that comes with knowing that you are His and He is yours. There is an assurance in that holy oath, that sacred declaration of the meaning of it all, *"that you should be Mine."*

There is no one better than The Creator to explain the identity and purpose of His creation. We don't have to wander, searching the wilderness for some hint of who we are. We don't need to spend years trying to figure ourselves out. We don't need to struggle to earn our worthiness. We don't need to escape our life to find ourselves. All we need to do is open our hearts to the Father who loves us and He will reveal to us who we are. We only need to step into His embrace to discover ourselves fully.

The truth is, we are not here in this time and place by accident. We are not alone in this life. God has meant, from the very beginning, to pursue us, to envelop us with His love. He intended to walk into our wilderness and show us the way to His promised land, His promised life, all along. It is His divine plan for us to discover all we are in the protection of His love. He wants us to discover the truth of who He knows us to be. He wants us to be lost in His love so fully that we find ourselves in Him.

Chapter *Two*

THE LEGEND OF US

Psalm 139:13 – 17
You formed my inward parts;
You covered me in my mother's womb
I will praise you for I am fearfully and wonder-
fully made
Marvelous are your works,
And that my soul knows very well
My frame was not hidden from You
When I was made in secret,
And skillfully wrought in the lowest parts of the
earth
Your eyes saw my substance being yet unformed
And in Your book they were all written
The days fashioned for me
When as yet there were none of them
How precious also are Your thoughts to me, O
God
How great is the sum of them

Every time I read these words I feel as though I am reading the prologue to a fairy tale or some great adventurous legend. My heart starts to race and my imagination is awakened. Each phrase and image builds upon the one before and it is almost more than I can bear. I am overwhelmed by all the possibilities that one so carefully and skillfully crafted could bring. I cannot wait to experience the rest of this magnificent story and then I realize that I don't have to wait. I am living this tale even now. This story is mine; it is the legend of me. And it is the legend of you.

Even though I have read and recited this passage thousands of times in my life, I still hear these words in my mother's voice and see them in her gently sweeping handwriting. While other children were read nursery rhymes as bedtime stories, I was recited this passage over and over again. *You formed my inward parts ... marvelous are your works... .* These flowing words captured my imagination and fed my soul from a very early age and I would spend hours puzzling out the meaning of all these poetic phrases. What I didn't realize then was that my mom was repeating these verses as much for her own comfort as for mine.

My mom's life didn't go exactly as she had planned, it wasn't even close to a fairy tale or legend of any kind. It was a survival story that she made up as she went along when all she could do was work hard and hope for the best. At the age of seventeen she made a decision that drastically altered the plans she had for her life. She fell for a popular, charismatic guy and she gave herself entirely to him. The relationship didn't last but it left a lasting impact, she became pregnant with me.

I'm sure God's perfect plan for my mom didn't include her becoming a teen mom but in her greatest moment of fear and confusion He made a way for her to find Him. He took her less than perfect decision and turned it around for His good. He brought comfort and help to my mom when she needed it the most and it came in the form of an invitation from my aunt to attend a Bible study.

So, the month before my mom turned eighteen she found Christ and the month after she turned eighteen I was born. Suddenly, she was a single teen mom, alone and scared. Nothing had turned out as she had planned yet she had hope because there was one truth that had wheedled its way into her heart. This one truth became bigger and more real to her than her circumstance and she held tight to it. *God created me and loves me more than I can ever comprehend.*

As a brand new Christian with a brand new baby, with the very earth beneath her feet shifting she found stability and security in these fourteen lines from the middle of the Bible that spoke to the truth that was growing in her heart. She didn't know what the future would hold, she wasn't sure of what life was going to be like for her and her infant daughter but she had faith that God knew. She clung desperately to that faith and she passed it along to me.

From my very beginning she was adamant that I understand that although she had made a mistake, I wasn't a mistake. She was determined that I know that God could take her lack of judgment and turn it into a significant piece of His divine design. She constantly reminded me that although she hadn't planned on getting pregnant at seventeen God had a plan for me. She did her all to claim my life for God and to frame it with His Word.

Nearly every birthday card I received from my mom contained all or part of this passage. She wrote it on Christmas cards, chore lists and highlighted it in every Bible I owned. When I was sad and lonely she would whisper these words to me and when I was searching for direction and meaning in my life this truth would echo through my heart. Whenever lies and doubt pushed in on me, when my own insecurities threatened to overwhelm me, these words gave me strength and reminded me of whose I am. These words became my own story, they became my personal beginning to remind me that God is with me until my end.

Read the passage again. Let the words wash over you. Meditate on the meaning, the weight of each phrase. Feel the power in this simple truth; God knew you before you were born. He hand-made you and planned for you. He thinks about you. Let that soak in.

He. Thinks. About. You.

The infinite God of the universe, the One who created the Heavens and the Earth, the One who breathed the world into existence, The One who is the beginning and the end thinks of *you.* He dreams of you. He desired you and so He created you! How marvelous is that?

But Creation was not the whole of His intention for us. He was not and is not content with mere existence for His masterpiece. He has so much more for each one of us. We weren't created as simple decorations for the earth. God intends for us to live a full, purposeful life. He wrote a book about each one of us!

I'm not sure if you have tried to write a novel but it's no easy thing. You don't just sit down and in an afternoon write a book. An author is an artist. They carefully craft each character as an individual. They give each character their own likes and dislikes, their own personalities, talents, hopes and desires. Each character has a specific purpose in the story. Once the characters are set it's time to weave the story.

Authors spend a lot of time thinking, plotting and imagining a whole world for their characters. They skillfully thread story lines and circumstances in and around their characters. They plan for their characters' whole lives; they know just how they want everything to play out. The crazy thing is most writers will confirm that their fictitious, purely fantasy–based, characters have a mind of their own. That often times the characters will do their own thing, stray from the plot, even as the author is writing the story.

I think that is sort of what happens with God and us. He has spent unimaginable time thinking, dreaming and creating each one of us. He has a master plan for each one of us, our own personal biography written before the fact, but because He has given us choice, the freedom to choose Him and His ways or not. So, sometimes we make a wrong decision and we stray from the plot. Our choice to do our own thing doesn't surprise God, He knows us so He knows what we'll do and He always makes a way for us to return to His divine story line. He redeems us. He loves us from the moment He first thought of us until the moment we walk into eternity with him and beyond.

He loves us. He *so* loves us.

PURPOSEFUL ART

Ephesians 2:10

For we are His workmanship, created in Christ Jesus for good works, which God prepared beforehand that we should walk in them.

The Eiffel Tower took two years to build. *The Last Supper* took 3 years to paint and The Sistine Chapel took 4 years. The Statue of Liberty took 11 years to complete and West Minister Abbey, which began construction in 1245, is still considered to be incomplete. These all are magnificent masterpieces, marvels of art and creativity, objects worthy of awe and wonder. All created with deliberation and intent.

Sometimes I try to imagine what it would have been like to be da Vinci, facing a blank wall or Michelangelo staring up at that great domed ceiling at the beginning of their projects. The possibilities for each space were endless. They could have painted anything. I wonder how long they thought, day-dreamed and planned for their masterpiece. I wonder if they realized then that with the first stroke of their brush they were creating a timeless masterpiece and stepping into history. Did they realize the significance of their work? Did they ever imagine that hundreds of years later people would still be celebrating what they created?

Ephesians 2:10 tells us that we are God's workmanship. Other translations use the terms handiwork or masterpiece instead of workmanship. Whatever the translation, the truth remains. We were each handmade by God. He is the artist and we are His masterpiece. We weren't an accident, some kind of scientific misstep that turned into something of value by chance. God put time, energy, thought and purpose into each one of His precious, created, handmade children. It wasn't by chance that He fashioned a being He that bore His image, His likeness and had His heart. We are no more a fortunate mishap than the *Mona Lisa* is an accidental art treasure.

If a master artist meditates, plans and imagines for hours, days or weeks in order to sculpt an image out of stone think of how much more God has thought and day-dreamed about us? His living, breathing works of art. God thought about each one of us, individually. He considered all that we could be and all that we would need to be just as He imagined.

Just as an artist carefully mixes paint to achieve just the right shades and hues so does God carefully measure out the different characteristics and talents He pours into each one of us. He sees to each detail while keeping The Big Picture firm in His mind's eye. He skillfully and patiently sculpts and molds our features, our very nature, until we reflect the exact image He dreamed of for us.

Unlike da Vinci and his contemporaries, God didn't create us as just a thing of beauty to hang on a gallery wall and be admired. He created us, His masterpieces, for a specific purpose. The gifts, talents and abilities that He placed in each one of us are there so that we may accomplish the good works He planned for us. He was very intentional in His creation of us and it breaks His heart when we fail to recognize our own magnificence, our own wonderful beauty in Him.

It is very common for people to feel lost, disconnected or useless. Many people walk through life haphazardly, believing the lie that they are the one extra person God created, the left over scraps hastily shoved into a human form and let loose without talent or function. They see other people living purposeful lives, accomplishing things and feeling fulfilled, they compare themselves and come up lacking. Over time they can become convinced that they are the one purposeless soul on the planet, that everyone else has all the talents, smarts, looks and abilities and they are the after birth, so to speak. This feeling is only reinforced when they try to be someone else, when they try to live out someone else's purpose, when they try to become an imitation of another work of art. It makes no more sense for us to try to emulate someone else's purpose than it does to use a sports car as a chicken coop. It'll do the job but it completely misses the fullness of its purpose.

God didn't create us and then think, "Hmm, now what am I going to do with this?" Right from the beginning, from the first idea of you, He had a whole plan for the great big life He wanted for you. He engineered you, designed you, hand crafted you for that specific life. There is nothing lacking in you for the plan He has for you. It is all there … waiting to be discovered in Him.

One day, the master sculptor, Michelangelo was asked how he imagined and then created *The Angel*. His reply was simple, yet profound, "I saw the angel in the marble and carved until I set him free." We are so like Michelangelo's angel. God has created us and we have to allow Him to chip away at everything that is not part of who He created. If we want to discover our full purpose, we have to trust Him to uncover all that He intended us to be and let go of our notions of what success and fulfillment look like.

Some people will read this and balk at the thought of some great puppet master in the sky manipulating them and forcing them into a life they don't want but it's not like that at all. God gave us our personalities, personal preferences and abilities because they fit perfectly with all that He designed for us. Who we are is a perfect compliment for all that He has created for us. But still we have a choice. We don't have to participate in His purpose. The choice to follow God's plan is ours.

Has anyone ever planned a surprise birthday party for you? In the moment the surprise is revealed you have a choice to make. You can get angry and refuse to participate or you can relax and enjoy the love and thoughtfulness that went into the plan. You can recognize the party for what it is, a celebration of you, or you can wallow in the untruth that you have been manipulated for someone else's selfish gain. You can bask in the fullness of love or you can shrink away in bitterness, the choice is entirely yours.

God's plan for us is kind of like that. It's there for us. Planned with love and consideration for our enjoyment. We're not forced into it, it's just there for us if we want it. God orchestrate every detail of His plan for us to suit our intricately handcrafted selves. He thought of everything we'd need, there is nothing lacking in Him. We just have to decide if we are going to participate.

I celebrate the good news in this verse. It took me a while to relax into His truth, that God thought of me, that He hand made me. But once I accepted that He has a purpose for me and that His purpose is far greater than anything I could dream up on my own I began to see how all the pieces of me are exactly what they need to be. As I allowed Him to chisel away anything that was not part of the masterpiece He had created me to be I could better see how perfect His plan for me really is and I could finally say, with confidence, "I'm here, in this time, in this place for a reason. I matter."

As do you …

You are God's own masterpiece created in the perfection of Jesus for a great big life of goodness that God, our loving and thoughtful Father day dreamed, planned for and prepared ahead of time that you would know your purpose and walk out all of your days in joy and confidence because of His love.

Chapter Four

FROM THE START

Genesis 1:26 & 27

*Then God said, "Let Us make man in Our image,
according to Our likeness." So God created
man in His own image, in the image of God He
created him, male and female, He created them.*

I've often struggled with the idea of being a woman. I know I am a woman but I've never much liked the company of women or girls for that matter. As a child, I found girls to be silly, mean and emotionally unstable. As a woman I've experienced far too many displays of the same childish behavior among my peers. I've had a hard time recognizing goodness in my own gender to the point of not really seeking out female friends. Acquaintances were fine but don't let any of them get too close. Casual encounters were safe but in order to keep the crazy drama at bay I felt I needed to limit my female contact.

I felt justified in my assessment of The Weaker Sex. From the beginning of time women have caused a lot of trouble, unnecessary drama and blatant meanness. Seriously, women were the source of most of the trouble in the Bible. Just look at Eve and Sarah and Leah, three very manipulative women. And don't even get me started on Delilah and Jezebel! Yep, women are bad news. It's best to just keep my head down and be as dude-like as possible, or so I thought until I tripped into an arena that I never planned on entering.

A while back, and completely out of the blue, I got involved in Women's Ministry at my church. One day I was alone in our church basement, setting up for Sunday School and listening to a teaching podcast when a friend showed up and asked me what I was doing. The next thing I knew I was leading a weekly women's meeting where we watched podcasts and discussed them. It was the last thing I intended to do but it was among the best things to ever happen to me.

Almost immediately, I began to see and value women differently. Getting to know the ladies who came out every week opened my eyes to a truth I should have recognized long ago. We are a work in progress, we are all doing our best to do our best. Through relationship with these magnificent women, I began to see the treasure that women are. I recognized that strength, loyalty, protection and nurturing are intrinsically part of the female nature and the things I previously disliked about women were never supposed to be part of our nature in the first place. God had designed us for community, care and cooperation, not for manipulation, contention and strife.

In preparation for the meetings each week I listen to dozens of podcasts from some of the best lady preachers of our age. The teaching and mentorship I have received from these Godly women through this medium has completely reshaped my perspective on my life, my faith and my place in this world. There have been many messages that have encouraged me and challenged me but none has impacted me more than the teaching that opened my heart to a truth I had never before realized; God created women on purpose.

The deliverer of this message was Lisa Bevere and I had never heard anyone like her. She said things like, "Women are not the problem, they are the answer" and "being a confident woman is not acting like a man." As I jumped head first into her teachings I began to see women in a completely different light, a God light. I read the Bible with a different understanding, from the perspective that women were part of God's plan from the beginning, and familiar verses came alive to me in a new way, verses like Genesis 1:26.

*... So God created man in His own image, in the image of God He created him, **male and female, He created them** ...*

In the very same sentence that God had the idea for man, He had the idea for woman. Before He breathed life into one, He had all eternity planned for the other. Woman was not an afterthought, created just to fill a void in man; she was half of the original thought. She was part of His plan all along. This idea rocked my world.

I began to think about men and women, the differences and the similarities. I began to ponder things through. If we were created in His image, both male and female, wouldn't male and female both be part of God's nature? If men have strengths and characteristics that are uniquely male given to them from the very nature of God, then wouldn't it be true that the things we claim as uniquely feminine are intrinsically part of God's nature also? If we, male and female, were created in His image then His image must hold the feminine as well as the masculine - right? And if that is the case then it stands to reason that God planned for us all, male and female, since the beginning of time.

And there it was. The IGIM that allowed all the pieces to click into place. There is no weaker sex because there's no weakness in God. No one is lesser than the other. No one is an after-thought; no one was created with the sole purpose of entertaining the other. One was not given the best traits and characteristics over the other. We, male and female, were created on purpose for a purpose since the beginning of time. We were created in unison, to complement each other, not to compete with or dominate each other. We are both, male and female, the image of our Father.

I was raised to know that God created me, the individual, on purpose but for the first time I realized that He created my gender on purpose and the purpose was not what I first thought. Women were not created just to keep men company. They were created as equal partners, as teammates. When God gave the instructions to be fruitful and multiply, to fill the earth and subdue it, to have dominion He wasn't just talking to Adam. Eve was there too. She was given the same instructions, the same responsibility, the same purpose. That was the key; God created male and female at the same time with a common purpose. Equal partners, helpmates. Not to be in competition but to help each other, each to bring out the strengths of the other. To be in relationship with each other and to work together.

When God said, "Let us create man in our image" He wasn't having a mental lapse and He wasn't talking to himself. He was referencing all parts of Himself; Father, Son and Spirit. He is one and He is three, working together. From the beginning He has been in community and since we are created in His image, in its entirety, we have been created to be in community. Our desire to belong and connect with others is God-given from the beginning of time. Our ability to partner with others, to be stronger together than we would be alone, is part of the very nature of God our Creator.

The very reason God created humans in the first place was out of a desire to be with someone, to have relationship with someone who wasn't heavenly obligated to be with Him. He wanted to be loved and sought after out of choice not force. He wanted us to want Him because He wanted us. And He wants that for us, too. Male and female. Created with a desire to be in community, in relationship, in partnership with each other.

Then God saw everything that He had made and indeed it was very good.

Chapter Five

DADDY'S GIRL

1 John 3:1

Behold what manner of love the Father has bestowed on us, that we should be called the children of God! Therefore the world does not know us, because it did not know Him.

My dad is kind of a quiet guy. He doesn't seek the limelight. He doesn't have a great talent that would gain him notice or fame. He's not highly educated and he doesn't have a lucrative, high-powered career. On the surface, he's just an ordinary guy. Nothing really remarkable about him at all.

But when you get close to him, when you step up and really look at him that's when you notice the treasure that he is; and it all starts with the twinkle in his eye. Within minutes of striking up a conversation with him you'll discover that he is anything but ordinary. He's actually kind of extraordinary.

He has a sharp, curious mind and mischievous streak that goes on for miles. He is quirky and a little bit funny. He is generous and unfailingly loyal. He loves his Jesus, his family and his Toronto Maple Leafs with unshakeable devotion (usually in that order but if the Leafs are in the playoffs all bets are off!). He is a Star Trek purest, a student of Sherlock Holmes and a patriotic, red and white through and through, Canadian to the core. But my favorite thing about my dad is that he chose me.

He married my mom when I was four years old and immediately adopted me as his own. He wasted no time and gave no second thought to making what was already in his heart official. Although I carry another man's DNA I have my dad's heart, I've had it from the beginning. He was my dad and I was his daughter and that's all there was to it. I was never his stepdaughter or his wife's daughter. I was always his; he made it as simple as that.

I was the one who made it complicated.

When I was thirteen years old I was told my whole story. My parents had never meant to hide it from me; they were waiting until I was old enough to understand the fullness of their love. They had hoped that the truth of the life I lived in this family would overshadow any rejection I might feel from being abandoned by one father before I was chosen by another. This was their hope, but the only thing my immature teenage mind heard was that I didn't belong, that I was separate somehow from the rest of my family.

Externally, I was still part of the family but a thought began that day that I struggled with into adulthood. *I started off this life belonging to another. I was adopted.* I turned the word adopted into something ugly and I began to wonder about this other dad. I wondered what he looked like, what his personality was like and if I was like him at all. I wondered what my life would have been like had he chosen to stay with me. I wondered what it was about me that was so unlovable that he had to leave.

I would watch my mom, dad and sister interact with each other and I would feel apart from them somehow. I felt as though they were the real family and I was an add-on, an extra bit they were stuck with. These thoughts swirled around my heart and threaded their way into too many situations where they cast shadows over occasions that should have been happy. Lies and assumptions twisted my heart and caused me to doubt the one true thing; my dad chose me and he loved me.

His love was constant. He never changed his mind or doubted whether I was really his or not. The moment he chose me it was a done deal in his heart and mind. I belonged to him. He gave me his name, called me his daughter and made me his family. He never thought of me as anyone other than entirely his own.

I can see that my doubt has hurt him, how those things that I have said out of my own confusion and pain have pierced his heart. I have been unfairly hard on him at times and yet he still loves me. He has never held my immature, hurtful actions against me. He still and always has called me his own, his sweetheart. He has always opened his arms and welcomed me as his own. His constant affection for me has helped me to understand the depth of love that my Heavenly Father has for me for He too has adopted me … and He's adopted you.

We were born apart from Him. We once belonged to another, a faithless deceiver who owned us but never loved us. The father of lies claimed us but even when we were apart from God, He saw us. He chose us, gave us His name and made us His family. His love is sure and yet our hearts doubt. We wonder how this Father can love us when our beginning was in another. We can't understand how this Father can love us so fully when we carry the DNA of another, one who is warped, twisted and diseased. How can this Good Father love us so completely when we come from one such as that? When we are of that make up?

The truth is we were stolen. We never did belong to the father of lies. He didn't create us, we don't carry his DNA. We have belonged to God from the very beginning. He created us, planned for us and loves us. When we were stolen He came for us, reclaimed us and adopted us back into His family. He brought us back to our rightful place as His children. We are His, plain and simple.

When we doubt or look back at what was once our life it hurts God's heart but it doesn't cancel His love for us. He knows the truth. He knows that His love is true and strong. He knows that anything the other father might offer is fleeting and leads to destruction. His concern is for us. His desire is to protect us, like the loving, kind and gentle Father He is.

The world doesn't understand this because they don't understand Him. If they have never been loved purely they can't even begin to comprehend the peace, security and life this kind of love brings. So they try to mock, tease and tempt us out of God's love. But if we stay the course, if we continue to believe and trust in His love the miraculous will happen. We will become more and more like Him. We will love like Him, protect like Him, serve like Him, live like Him. We will begin to resemble Him so strongly that people won't know where He ends and we begin. His love will wipe out any trace of that other father and we will be fully and wholly His.

Recently, an acquaintance saw a picture of my dad and me together and remarked how much we look alike. I thanked her and chuckled to myself. All through my life people have commented how much I'm like my dad and for years I would try to explain how that was impossible. I would squirm under the mention of this connection because I thought it was false. But now I am thrilled to hear that I am like him because I have his heart and he has mine. It is true that I am like him, that his love has influenced me so greatly that I resemble him. I have been adopted twice and both of my dads love me and call me their own.

O what manner of love!

THE ONE WHO JESUS LOVES

John 21:20 & 24

...the disciple whom Jesus loved ... This is the disciple who testifies of these things and who wrote these things and we know that his testimony is true

I'm not really a baby person. I'm not one of those people who get all worked up over infants. I mean, they're all right but I prefer kids once they have a few skills under their belts and can keep their bodily fluids to themselves. There are a few exceptions to this rule though. I have one sister and my one sister has one daughter, my only niece, Bizzy, and this kid is most definitely an exception.

Since before Bizzy was born I have done my all to convince, cajole and bribe my way into the number one spot of her affections. My sole goal and desire when it comes to my niece is to be her favorite. I spent hours talking to my sister's baby bump, willing the baby to like me best. Once Bizzy was born I became a total baby hog. I went with the theory that if I held her all the time she wouldn't know anyone else and if I were the only person she knew I'd have to be her favorite.

All of my hard work seemed to be paying off when she was about a year old, because if I asked her who her favorite was she'd point to me. Sweet victory! But that didn't last long. Now that she's a little older she's wise to my schemes and she toys with me. I ask her who her favorite is and she names my daughter or she tells me that her fake aunt (a family friend) is her favorite or that I can be her favorite just for an hour or so. She has me jumping through hoops for the honor of being in that number one spot, for the joy of holding the title of 'Bizzy's Favorite' or 'The One who Bizzy Favors Above All Else.' Honestly, I'd do almost anything to get that prize!

Recently, I read through the book of John and noticed a curious thing. John, who wrote the book, refers to himself as 'the one who Jesus loves.' My first instinct upon reading this was to laugh. I mean, seriously, I guess when you're the one writing the story you can say whatever you'd like about yourself. But when I thought about it a little more I began to wonder what it was exactly about John that Jesus loved so much. How did John get that favored title out of the twelve disciples? How did John get himself noticed and loved above the multitudes? And ... hey! I thought that God didn't have favorites!

It's true, Acts 10:34 has Peter saying that, in his best under-standing, God didn't show partiality, that no matter who you are and where you're from God accepts you. So if that is true, if God doesn't play favorites then John can't be the only one Jesus loved, right? I mean, there have to be others. What about Thomas and Peter and Judas and the rest of the guys? Didn't Jesus love all of them, too? If so, why aren't they known as Thomas the beloved and Peter the beloved and Judas the beloved? Why are they known for doubting, denying and betraying instead?

When Jesus chose His disciples He wasn't choosing minions, He was choosing friends. These guys hung out with Him 24/7. Wherever Jesus went, so went The Twelve. They ate, slept and lived together. He *liked* all of them. He saw value in each one of them and offered all of them the same measure of friendship. His heart was open to each one of them and He desired to know them each as individuals. Jesus was the same with each of them. It was each of them who responded differently to Him. It's that individual response that made John the beloved and Judas the betrayer. The difference was them, not Him.

I think the issue was in how each one saw themselves and the truth they accepted about their relationship with Jesus. Something in John readily accepted that Jesus chose him, Jesus loved him and that was all he needed. He was comfortable with the worthiness that reflected back to him through his friendship with Jesus. He didn't doubt it, he didn't try to earn it. He just accepted Jesus' love as is. His heart was open to receive all that Jesus had for him. Thomas, Peter and Judas not so much.

Those three disciples, for different reasons and at different times, squirmed under the blanket of holiness that Jesus tried to envelop them in. They questioned the love and rejected the friendship offered to them. They couldn't believe that it all was as simple as just believing. They grappled with the same question of worthiness that many of us do. They struggled to find a way to earn Jesus' love and therefore a place in His kingdom. Sound familiar?

God has filled His Word with descriptions and examples of who He says we are. He calls us His own (Galatians 4:6), chosen (2 Thessalonians 2:13) and holy (1 Peter 2:9) but is that how we see ourselves? We limit Jesus' love for us by the truth we know of ourselves. We define this truth based on our past thoughts and behavior. And most often the definition we accept of ourselves is the one we can bear, the one we can accept in light of our imperfections, our failings, our sin. But, Beloved, that's not how God sees us at all!

He doesn't measure His love based on our worthiness. He doesn't add and subtract His affection in relation to our behavior. His love just *is*. We don't have to earn it. We couldn't earn it if we tried. He offers it freely and all we have to do is freely accept it, accept Him. It's as simple as believing the truth that God loves us. He *so* loves us that He sent His willing Son to sacrifice His own life so that we might be able to have relationship with Him. God has chosen us. He has created us. He has called us into a magnificent life with Him. He has made us worthy and holy and just. He loves us. We are the one Jesus loves!

Imagine owning that definition of yourself. Picture introducing yourself just that way. You walk into a room full of strangers, such as at a party or something, and confidently walk up to a group of people gathered by the guacamole. You smile, extend your hand and say, "Hi, I'm Taylor, the one who Jesus loves." And they reply back, "Nice to meet you Taylor, I'm Sylvia, the one who Jesus loves and this is my friend Braden, also the one who Jesus loves." What if we all claimed that love as our own? What if we simply believed in the truth of that love?

But just like Judas, Peter and Thomas we all too often get in our own way. We think wealth, power or popularity will attract His love or grand gestures and radical declarations will earn it. When none of these ploys work we doubt in the reality of His love.

We look at love from our human, earthly perspective and judge it by the same merits as we give love. Although Jesus is entirely human He is also entirely God. His love does not know the limits and restrictions of our earthly love. He *is* love. His love is holy, limitless and endless. It is this love that He offers to us. We don't have to convince, cajole or bribe Jesus to love us. He just does. We are His Beloved. We are the ones Jesus loves. We are the ones.

Chapter Seven

A DIVINE LOVE LETTER

2 Timothy 3:16

All Scripture is given by inspiration of God, and is profitable for doctrine, for reproof, for correction, for instruction in righteousness, that the man of God may be complete, thoroughly equipped for every good work.

Mr. Awesome and I have a unique love story that sparks more than a few questions any time we share it. We never dated. Not one date, not one kiss, not one hint of a romance. We friended and then we fianced. It was the last thing I expected yet, somehow, it was the very thing I was waiting for; He was the one I had been waiting for.

When Mr. Awesome and I first made the move from friends to fiancés we were living three provinces apart. I left Manitoba to attend school in British Columbia and we were 'just friends.' Four weeks later he called me from Manitoba and told me we should get married. Another month later I was on a plane heading back home to my new fiancé.

Before all this flying halfway across the country and engagement stuff happened we were friends. Best friends. I knew him better than just about anyone and vice-versa. We had spent a lot of time together, talking, hanging out and getting to know each other. I knew he preferred Pepsi over Coke, didn't care for spectator sports or anything messy and had once been arrested for breaking into a school. He knew that I loved coffee and classic literature, could quote every line in *The Princess Bride* and was once suspended from private Christian school for drinking alcohol on school property. We both enjoyed watching movies, being in the wilderness and drinking slurpees. We knew each other, but during those two months apart while I was away at school, we got to know each other in a whole different way. We started writing letters to each other.

The first letter I received from Mr. Awesome was three days after I arrived at school. From then on he sent me a letter about every second day. In these letters I began to understand his spirit in a completely different way. He wrote freely of his dreams and his hopes. He wrote of childhood memories and plans for the future. He wrote poems and quoted song lyrics. It was in his letters that he first told me he loved me.

Although I spoke to him on the phone nearly every day, I couldn't wait to receive his letters because it was in his written word that I got to see right into his heart. It was in the quiet moments of reading and rereading his words that I grew to know him and love him and trust him. When we were thousands of miles apart, he laid the foundation to our relationship with his words and when I was lonely, homesick or flooded with doubts, I could open one of his letters and know that I was his and he was mine and it was only a matter of time until we would be together again.

My relationship with God has been very similar. I've known Him for a long time. He has long been my Friend, Protector,

Comfort, Encourager and my Father. I've spent time with Him. I've talked with Him. I've spent time with His other friends and they've told me about Him. Most of my life I have enjoyed a comfortable relationship with Him but I have had glimpses of a much more intimate relationship. I've had a taste of what real friendship with God is meant to be and now I can't go back to the way things used to be. I've read His Word and I've seen His very heart. I now know that He is mine and I am His. Fully and Completely.

A while ago I purposed to do something I'd never done before: read the entire Bible. Every word. I found a Bible reading plan that looked good and I dove right in. I had expected to read the same old stories and letters that I had been taught since childhood. I expected to be a little bit bored as I read through the Old Testament and a little bit less bored as I read through the New Testament. I expected this new routine to be a bit of a chore but I was determined nonetheless. What I didn't expect was to completely fall in love with God and His Word in a totally new and different way. I didn't expect these same old stories and letters to breathe new life into my soul.

The writer of Hebrews tells us that the word of God is living and active (Hebrews 4:12), and it is. I have experienced first-hand how some of the same old scriptures I'd memorized in childhood have come alive to me in a completely different way. There are passages I have read over and over again and still they seem new to me and then there are other verses that I'd swear are new to the Bible, but in truth, they're just new to me. With each new verse and chapter I read I see the heart of God in a unique and intimate way. I am getting love drunk on the Bible as I discover a different facet to my Heavenly Father with each turn of the page.

In Genesis He is our Creator. In Exodus He is our Deliverer. In Ruth He is our Protector. In Psalms He is our Song. In Isaiah He is our Hope for the future. In Jonah He is our second chance. In Matthew He is our Savior King. In Luke He is our Healer. In Acts He is our Comforter. In Ephesians He is our Teacher. In Revelation He is our Bridegroom. He is all this and so much more.

Every word in the Bible is inspired by the Spirit of God. It is His divine love letter to us, His children. He wrote it so that we might know Him and discover His heart intimately. He wants us to read it, to know it so well that it is written in our hearts. It is in these God-inspired words that we find everything we need to live the life He has imagined for us. It is within the pages of the Bible that we get to know Him, His hopes, dreams and expectations. It's in these holy, beautiful words that we learn about His love for us. And it is through this knowledge and heart understanding of His nature that we can speak confidently of who He is and therefore bring others into relationship with Him.

Since I began to read the Bible daily, I have seen a total change in my relationship with God, which has led to a change in my relationship with others. I understand now that His love is all-encompassing, His grace is never-ending and His hope is eternal. Knowing this has made it easier for me to extend this same love, grace and hope to those in my world. I understand better the depth of the forgiveness I've been given and feel compelled to give the same measure of forgiveness. I see the power of God's community in action and I want to be part of that community known as His Church. I experience His blessings and I can't help but share them with others.

Just like reading those letters from Mr. Awesome shaped my love and relationship with him, so reading the Bible shapes my love and relationship with God. It was through reading the intimate words of his heart that I came to love Mr. Awesome and it is the same yet so much more with God. It is through reading the Word of God that I've come to understand that He has been waiting for me to find Him, to know Him and to love Him. He has been waiting for me to accept His love and walk into His embrace. He has been waiting for me to lose myself in Him so that He can find me. He's been waiting for me to discover His heart in the love letter He wrote just for me.

He has been waiting for me.

Section

Two

He is Mine

Belonging is a two-way street. One claims another but the one claimed has to consent or the relationship is not one of loving protection but one of domination. And that's not how God operates.

God claimed me. He called me His own. He offered love, protection, guidance and help. He offered His name, His benefits and His blessing. He offered but I had to accept. I had to reciprocate the claim before it really meant something, before it could alter my life. I had to accept what God was offering and I had to make Him mine in return.

When I was growing up in the church, I heard the saying, "God doesn't have grandkids," and it confused me. I reasoned that if my parents were God's kids then of course I was God's grandkid. It wasn't until I hit my older teens years that I understood the sentiment behind the phrase.

Spiritually, I coasted through my childhood and early teen years. My parents sent me to a private Christian school, to Sunday school, to youth group, to youth camp and Sunday morning church services were always a family event. I was thoroughly churched by my folks until the age of fourteen. It was then that my youth pastors moved away and I fell out of sync with The Church Machine. I had aged out of Sunday school, I was in my final year of private school and I didn't fit in with the current youth group crowd. I started skipping youth and distancing myself from my 'church' friends. Church began to feel like a thing we did and not who I was. But that changed the night I was kidnapped.

One Friday night, as I was zoning out in front of the TV, my front door banged open and I was hauled off the couch and shoved into a car. I was barefoot, couch-headed and sloppy t-shirted but

I was being dragged out of the house nonetheless. The kidnapper was my cousin and with the help of her friends she got me to her youth group. She had been inviting me for weeks but I kept making excuses as to why I couldn't attend. There would be no more excuses from this point on.

It was during the four years I spent at this youth group that I learned that my relationship with God was my responsibility. I couldn't be His grandkid, I had to become His child. That was the only role He was offering.

My youth pastor challenged me to read my Bible, to know what God said about me, to use the gifts and talents He had given me to reach out, to serve and to bring others into relationship with God. He pushed me to let God mess with me. He supported me through my failures and gave me opportunities to succeed and every step of the way my youth pastor reminded me that God had offered family to me but it was my decision, daily, whether I was going to accept it or not.

I accepted. I still accept it. I belong to God. I am His.

And He is Mine.

Chapter **Eight**

BROUGHT NEAR

Ephesians 2:13

But now in Christ Jesus you who once were far off have been brought near by the blood of Christ.

I love the book of Ephesians. There is a poetry and flow of the words that makes my heart sing. The apostle Paul weaves his words of community, mystery and wisdom around the central theme, the core truth of Jesus' love for us. His words spark my imagination and speak to my very heart. The truth he writes brings comfort and peace and a hope beyond measure. It's easy to get lost in this world of Jesus' enduring love and forget about what our reality was before Jesus came.

I've done some reading in Leviticus, Numbers and Deuteronomy lately. I've decided to read the Bible all the way through so there's no way around it. These books are in there so I have to read them. They're not exactly the 'feel good' reads of the

Bible so I wasn't super thrilled when I got to them. In retrospect, though, I'm glad I took the time to slog through them.

Reading these Books of the Law painted a very vivid picture for me of just how far from God we were before Jesus. It was within the laws of what was that I began to fully appreciate the gift of what is. Chapter after chapter in these books is dedicated to the detailed description of the rules and sacrifices priests had to follow just so a select few could encounter God. Not a select few from the general population but a select few priests. God's holiness was, and is, a severe thing, not to be taken lightly. The vast majority of the children of Israel, though forgiven through sacrifice, could not get near to God because they were unable to get clean enough to survive His holiness. Their sacrifices were only a temporary fix for an eternal problem. It's true that this atonement through sacrifice brought these select few closer to God than any had been since Adam and Eve bit the apple, but it was still a far cry from the relationship that God yearned for.

It was out of this desire to reestablish relationship with the people He created, the people who He loved, that God instructed Moses to build the tabernacle. This was to be a place for God to be near His people but still, not too near, not fatally near.

God told Moses to build the tabernacle with three sections; a courtyard, a sanctuary and another space known as The Holy of Holies. It was in that final space that the presence of God would dwell but most people would never make it past the courtyard. He was near –er but not actually with the people He loved so much. He was closer than He had been in generations but still not close enough to really know and be known. It would be like visiting your parents at their house but not being allowed to go any further than the front yard. They are sitting inside and you are outside. You can yell through the window at them and they can hear you but it's not an ideal circumstance. Conversation would be difficult and a lot of work and your relationship would suffer.

That was God and us. Since the Garden of Eden we have been stuck, separated from The One who created us with the purpose of being in relationship with Him. We couldn't get near to Him because of our sin and He wouldn't dare approach us because He knew that His holiness was more than we could bear. So there we sat, for generations, in the front yard, while He sat in the house. Both of us longing to be with the other but neither able to bridge the gap.

Then Jesus came. The loving sacrifice of His life for ours created a tidal wave of His cleansing, healing blood that washed over us, covering our sin and carrying us right into the very house of our Father. We were able to ride the wave of Jesus' love right into the presence of God. Our Father was finally able to wrap His arms around us and draw us near. He was finally able to be the hands-on Dad we needed and we were able to find comfort and safety in His protection and guidance.

There are few things that make you feel more helpless as a parent than watching your child struggle or step into the path of danger when you are too far away to help. When our youngest son was about 18 months old we went to spend time with our family in Alberta. As we did on every visit, we took a couple of days to explore Banff and the surrounding area. We picnicked in the meadow on Mount Norquay, walked around the gardens at Canada House and splashed in the cool waters of the Bow River. We were making memories and I was capturing as many of these memories on film as possible.

At the river, while I was snapping pictures of the kids splashing and playing, Mr. Awesome waded out into deeper waters with Dude. I had taken a few beautiful pictures of wee Mischief playing with rocks on the shore and then turned to take a few of Crafty as she attempted to pick rocks out of the river without actually getting wet. Still laughing at the antics of my silly girl, I trained my camera on Mr. Awesome and Dude, who were about forty feet away, gingerly making their way across the rocky-bottomed river. I was about to snap the picture when I glanced down to where Mischief was playing, just to make sure he was still within reach, but he wasn't there.

I'd only looked away from him for a minute or so but in that brief span of time Mischief had wandered off. I glanced down the beach and towards the parking lot but I couldn't see him. Then I turned back to the water, scanning the shallows, and spotted him. Mischief was halfway between where I was on the beach and where Mr. Awesome was in the water. But in the moment I saw him, he disappeared again. My heart dropped to my feet and cemented me in place for a moment as I watched my baby struggle against the cold mountain waters to find his feet.

Mr. Awesome must have seen the look on my face and put two and two together. Before I could even think to respond, he had already crossed the distance and rescued Mischief. As Mr. Awesome rushed toward me, with our blue-lipped, but breathing, boy in his arms, an indescribable sense of relief washed over me; my boy would soon be in my arms. Safe.

Mischief recovered quickly but I have never forgotten that feeling of utter helplessness and despair that filled my heart as I watched him struggle for life outside my reach. I was completely undone at the thought of losing my precious boy. This experience brought a new level of understanding to me about the Father heart of God. If the limits of my human heart could feel that measure of grief how much more did the heart of Father God ache, as He watched His children flounder and struggle for generations, outside His grasp? How could He just stand by and watch the ones He so loved perish? How could He stand to lose us?

He couldn't. He sent Jesus to rescue us, to bring us to Him. We are no longer fighting for life at a distance. Jesus swept through eternity, through our own doubting hearts, and saved us. He cleared a path through every sinful obstacle, every thought and action that kept us from our Father, and carried us right to the throne of God. He kicked open the door and tore down the curtain that separated us from the Father who loves us. We no longer have to struggle on our own at a distance from Him. God is within our reach and better still, we are within His.

Chapter *Nine*

TRANSFORMED IN LOVE

Romans 5:6-8

For when we were still sinners without strength in due time Christ died for the ungodly. For scarcely for a righteous man will one die; yet perhaps for a good man someone would even dare to die. But God demonstrates His own love toward us, in that while we were still sinners, Christ died for us.

There is little that stirs emotion and tugs at the heart like a good story. Action, adventure, mystery and suspense all grab our attention and make our hearts race. But it's a sacrificial love story that really gets us every time. Who didn't get a little weepy when Jack slipped away under the cold Atlantic waters while Rose was rescued or when Captain Miller, shot and dying, whispers to Private Ryan "earn this." Don't get me started on the ugly cry that occurs every time I see The Beast die in Belle's arms after battling Gaston.

One person loving another enough to die in their place is considered to be the ultimate declaration of affection and sacrifice. The heroes in these incredible stories are usually motivated by duty, honor, patriotism and love. Those saved from death are sympathetic characters who are worthy of being saved; mothers, best friends, lovers and children. We can all cheer for the worthy being saved but not so much for the unworthy.

No one wants to see the unjust being saved in place of the just. It messes with our sense of right and wrong but in truth this is our story. We are the undeserving ones who were saved while The Hero perished. We get to live free while Another paid the ultimate price. It's the truth of salvation and it makes no sense to our way of reasoning. The idea of the divine dying for the earthly is beyond our understanding because our understanding is earthly. We comprehend the world from our human perspective but God designed the world from His divine understanding. That's the gap in our ability to fully grasp the things of God.

When we look at things from our human perspective nothing about God or how He operates makes sense to us. Just look at Jesus. His life and ministry plays out in a string of counter-intuitive events. From birth to death to resurrection, none of it makes sense. It certainly isn't believable when we try to puzzle it out with our natural minds, but when we open our hearts to the truth of the story we might see things from The Author's perspective.

Choosing a thirteen-year-old girl to mother the Messiah just seems like a recipe for disaster. Most thirteen-year-olds can't even keep track of their iPods never mind feeding, caring and nurturing a baby. Our understanding of teens is limited to what we see externally - their childishness, their lack of responsibility, their frivolity, but The Author sees the heart and the possibilities. We see an immature teenager but He sees a righteous young woman with childlike faith - enough to believe what God says is true. He sees an opportunity for the glorious to shine through the simple and this perspective is one that was passed from Father to Son.

During His time ministering on this earth Jesus mixed and met with all sorts of people. He didn't care about social standing, wealth or position. He didn't measure how being seen with certain people would affect His reputation and He certainly didn't care what people thought of how He brought about the miraculous change that was needed in the lives of those with whom He interacted with. Jesus did what was right in the moment, from His heavenly, eternal perspective, and it defied our human sense every time.

He spat in a blind man's eye, opened the tomb of a dead guy and offered a child's snack to 5,000 hungry men. None of it makes sense. It's ridiculous and foolish and completely useless. But Jesus didn't see things that way.

He saw the blind man as an opportunity to show how God can take nothing and turn it into the miraculous. He opened Lazarus' tomb to prove that even death cannot stop the power of His love. He used the small lunch of a boy to feed the multitudes to remind us that He can turn our everyday ordinary lives into an occasion to celebrate His abundance.

When we look at things from God's perspective the absurd becomes logical. And His sacrifice, Jesus taking our sin and disobedience and dying in our place, is exactly that, divinely logical and lovely. Before Jesus we were without God, alone and separated, and the only solution to this situation was to, somehow, be with God. The only way for this to happen, for the earthly to be in relationship with the divine, was for love to step in.

Jesus dying in our place has absolutely nothing to do with our worthiness or goodness. God did not sacrifice Jesus to make us worthy. He sacrificed Jesus so that He, God our Father, could be in relationship with us. He sacrificed Jesus because He loved us, loves us still and wants to know us. He wants to be part of our everyday living, working, eating, and breathing lives. He wants to be near us and wants us to be near Him, but this closeness came at a cost. Jesus, who was man and God, had to bridge the gap between human and Holy so that we could meet God face to face.

It was all done out of love and for relationship. Becoming worthy, righteous and holy is a by-product of this act of love, not the goal.

It's like getting married. If you marry someone with the mind set that you can change him or her, your relationship with be a disaster from the get go. You will be discontent and dissatisfied with who they are and they will be miserable and feel inadequate all the time. But when you marry someone because you love him or her your relationship will flourish. They will bask in the affection and respect that you freely give and contentment, joy and security will envelop both of you. This creates the perfect conditions for natural growth and change. It is in the safety of this accepting and forgiving relationship that love abounds and transformation is free to occur. Being changed by love is a by-product of a healthy marriage, not the goal just as our holiness is a by-product of the Father's love, not the goal.

When we were still ungodly, lost sinners God loved us. He didn't see us and think, "Some day, that person is going to be holy enough for me to love." He sees us and says, "Today, this day, this is the person I love!" He loves *us*, not what we might one day become but who we are, now.

When we understand that all Jesus did for us is because of His love, because of who He is and not because of any realized or potential goodness in us, we can relax into His love. We can surrender our weakness to His strength; we can allow His affection for us to draw us near, envelop us, and protect us. We can release the pressure we feel to deserve what is beyond our capacity to earn. We can just exhale and be in the love of our Father.

There is freedom in being loved like this. All pretences and facades can be dropped. All struggles to understand or earn this affection can be abandoned because, in the end, it is us who God desires, not a holy version of us. Us. As we are. In this moment. That's it. We are all He requires us to be because His love has made us so. Now that is a magnificent love story!

Chapter *Ten*

COLLECTED MOMENTS

Philippians 4:8

*Finally brethren, whatever things are true, what-
ever things are noble, whatever things are just,
whatever things are of good report, if there is any
virtue, if there is anything praiseworthy – meditate on these things.*

Once a week I have the privilege of facilitating a Bible study
for the women in my community. During one of these morning
meetings we were talking about how God walks us through different trials and circumstances in our lives and I was telling the
ladies that God can teach us something about His nature in every
situation He walks us through. I was explaining that these little
nuggets of wisdom and peace are just there, waiting for us to pick
them up and claim them as our own when Holy Spirit spoke to
my heart and pointed out a truth I had been trying to ignore.

"Yeah, but you've picked up things along the way that you were never meant to touch."

In an instant I had a mental picture of a long and twisting dirt road. The road was full of debris that made it difficult to see a clear path. All along the side of the road, within easy reach, were neatly wrapped packages and brightly colored gift bags. I was in the middle of the road, slowly making my way forward with great difficulty. The path wasn't clear and I was weighed down by all the things I was carrying. I had a few of the colorful bags in hand but mostly, I was burdened with heavy rocks and sharp fragments that were cutting into my skin and leaving me bruised and sore.

I knew that some of the things I was holding I had only picked up to move out of the way. I also got the sense that there was much more that I had no intention of letting go of, even though I was scarred and bleeding from the jagged edges. My arms had become full, so full of garbage, that I had no room or strength to pick up the gifts beside the road, no matter how desperately I wanted to. I just kept stumbling forward blindly, as unable to let go of what was hurting me as I was unable to pick up the gifts that I knew were mine.

"You have gathered things along this journey that you were never meant to touch. You have held these useless items as proof to use against your husband, proof that he doesn't love you, proof that his promises are false. As you've been collecting your proof you've missed out on the gifts that I've laid out for you. Now, you have a choice. You can either keep collecting your proof so you will have it at the ready for when he fails you. Oh yes, he will fail you; he is only human. Or you can drop the garbage, heal and free yourself to receive all the good things I have prepared for you. For I am good. I am God and I will never fail you. What are you going to do?"

This all happened in a split second in my mind and heart. There was no audible voice and the ladies in the room had no idea that I had just had this encounter with God. Nevertheless, I knew what I had seen and heard in my spirit was genuine. I knew that

God was dealing with me in a very real way with an issue I had tried so hard to ignore for so long.

Somewhere along the way I had convinced myself that Mr. Awesome was only tolerating me, biding his time until he could make a clean break. I had collected things – words said in anger, perceived slights and thoughtless acts – to prove that his love wasn't true. It didn't matter how much he showered me with affection, how many words of love and respect he spoke, in my heart I knew that he was only going through the motions and I had my collection to prove it.

There was never a time that I consciously decided to start this painful collection. Looking back, I think that it sort of snuck up on me during the early days of our marriage, when I was too insecure and immature to talk about my issues and my fears. Instead I would replay conversations we'd had or looks he'd given me over and over, trying to decipher any hidden meanings or veiled insults. When I didn't know what to make of these incidents I would store them away in my memory, holding them tight in case they were indicators of my worst fear, that he didn't really love me, after all.

I knew that what I was doing was wrong and unhealthy. I knew that I was creating a prison and locking myself in. In my happiest moments I realized that my thought life was out of control and I was crazy to distrust this man who had never been anything but true, loving and loyal. I would pray and ask God to help me to forget all these hurts but I never once considered letting go of them myself. I would go for months and sometimes years without thinking of my collection but eventually something would happen to bring all those hidden worries to the forefront of my mind and it would take me ages to suppress them all again. Each time this happened, it left scars on our relationship and it tainted my perception of Mr. Awesome and the truth of his love and commitment.

Soon after my moment with Holy Spirit, I sat down with Mr. Awesome and told him all about what I had seen and what I felt

God was speaking to me. I told him that it was true; I had been collecting proof to use against him. I explained how I had become trapped in my own creation of distrust and that I felt as though I had robbed us of so many years of full love and partnership. My tears flowed freely as I asked his forgiveness for holding against him things he had never done.

Long after I had spoken my last word I continued to cry tears of relief, humility and healing. Mr. Awesome held me and whispered words of love and affirmation to me. I felt, and continue to feel, so blessed to have a Father God who loves me enough to gently correct me and a husband who unconditionally loves me in, and through, all of my brokenness.

What I understand now, that I never had before, is that in all of our relationships we have a choice. We can do as I did and focus on the negative, hurtful and thoughtless moments or we can focus on the true, good and life-giving moments. We can prepare ourselves for the moment we'll be let down or we can fill ourselves with the moments of love and joy so that when we are let down we will be carried through. What we fill our mind with will fill our heart and it is what is in our heart that sustains us, or overwhelms us, when trying times come.

It's also important to remember that friendship, relationship with the people in our life, is a gift from God but it is not meant to take the place of our relationship with Him. God gives us people to love and to be loved by, to demonstrate His love for us, not to replace it. When we put unrealistic expectations on people we set them up to disappoint us. If all of our happiness, security and well-being rests on the shoulders of our loved ones they will buckle under the weight to be sure. A mere human was never meant to carry such a load. When we put God first and focus on His goodness our joy will be secure and our heart will be safe. When we fill our hearts and minds with all that is true, noble, just, good, virtuous and praiseworthy about our relationships, they will flourish.

Chapter *Eleven*

BECAUSE OF WHO HE IS

Psalm 23:3

He restores my soul; He leads me in the paths of righteousness for His name's sake.

I remember studying Psalm 23 in grade school. I think I was in the fourth grade when I memorized this passage and since then it has been imprinted on my heart. It's one of those passages that just sort of sticks with you. It's familiar, comfortable and predictable. No surprises here.

Recently, I read this passage again and saw something I had never seen before, a semicolon, and it changed my whole understanding of this verse. Being a bit of a grammar geek, nothing thrills me more than a well-written sentence or properly placed punctuation but this was something more than that. This semicolon gave an entirely different meaning to this passage for me. This little piece of punctuation changed my understanding of my righteousness.

It had been years since I had actually read Psalm 23. Whenever a pastor would reference it in a sermon I would just recall it from memory, no need to flip all those pages to read something I already knew so well. I was tempted to do the same thing the day this passage came up on my Bible reading plan. I was just going to skip reading what I already knew and move on to something new, something fresh, something that wasn't cliché. But I had promised myself to read every word of the Bible, and I had already slogged through a mess of begats, so why now skip this wee psalm?

As I started the passage I bristled a little at the all-too-familiar, sappy imagery of green pastures and still waters but then verse 3 grabbed my attention. Although I knew this passage well, I had missed the meaning; that one little semicolon flipped the switch of my understanding and suddenly, I got it. I had an IGIM.

A semicolon is used to tie two related ideas together. The two ideas can stand as independent thoughts and sentences but when a writer wants to link the ideas, wants to show the relationship between the thoughts, a semicolon is used.

He restores my soul; He leads me in the paths of righteousness.

He doesn't restore my soul. Period. And then lead me in paths of righteousness. He restores my soul *by* leading me in paths of righteousness. The two are connected. Leading and restoring. It is following in His righteous footsteps that restores my soul. It is seeking His goodness that heals my heart. I find my perfect wholeness in Him.

There have been times in my life that I didn't want to do what God asked of me. I didn't want to be inconvenienced or made to look foolish. I didn't understand what He was asking or I didn't trust Him that everything would turn out well. Whatever the reason, I chose to walk my own path and the further I got from His plan the more 'off' everything felt. Great calamity and destruction didn't overwhelm me in my disobedience but internally something felt out of sync. Inside my heart the rhythm of my life was off.

For instance, a while ago I was asked to attend a women's conference with some ladies from my church. I knew that I was supposed to go. I felt God nudging my spirit and piece by piece things came together to make it easy for me to go but I didn't want to. I didn't want to get on a bus with 30 women and drive 8 hours. I didn't want to share a room with someone I hardly knew. I didn't want to be inconvenienced into relationship with a bunch of strangers so I didn't go. I made an excuse and bowed out.

The morning that the gals all left for the conference I laid in my bed and pulled the covers over my head. I knew that I was being disobedient to what God had planned. I knew and I was hiding. And I continued to hide for months. I avoided the lady who organized the event. I attempted to side-step any conversation about the conference and I tried desperately to pull away from anything to do with the women's ministry. I put a lot of time, thought and energy into avoiding what I knew God was asking of me and I ended up miserable and exhausted. And I felt apart from God.

When I finally recognized what I was doing, and the amount of effort I was putting into maintaining my disobedience, I felt like an idiot. I realized that God wasn't trying to punish me with an all-expenses-paid, kid-free weekend with a great group of women. He was trying to open the door to relationship for me with the women in my community. He was trying to introduce me to the next thing He had for me to do and I missed it because of my own stubbornness and stupidity. The moment I repented and turned back to God things began to shift. When I returned to His path, His righteous way, my soul became whole and peaceful once again.

Understanding how my soul is restored led me to understand the next part of this verse in a different way. When I first memorized this passage I thought the verse read 'For His namesake' and I understood it to mean that He makes us righteous for Jesus' benefit. I thought that God expected us to be righteous because He sacrificed His son, like we owed Him a life of holiness because He did us the favor of sacrificing His Son in our place. But again, punctuation changes everything and this time the credit goes to the apostrophe.

For His name's sake

What is His name? What are the names we know God by? Almighty. Author. Perfector. Holy. Deliverer. Shepherd. Redeemer. Father. Because He is all of these things, and so much more, He meets us where we are and leads us into relationship with Him. He comes to us, not because we owe Him but because He is who He is.

It is the very nature of God to guide, protect, save and restore. He specializes in taking the broken and making something beautiful from them. He doesn't expect the broken to make their way to Him. No, He goes out looking for the broken, the lost and the hurting. He finds them and He lovingly and patiently leads them into relationship with Him. He gently restores their souls with His love and kindness.

When I admitted to God, and to myself, that I had refused to do what God asked of me, when I returned to the path He had set before me, God didn't punish me. He didn't shame me. He didn't require me to find a way to make it up to Him. He lovingly accepted my apology and provided a way for me to get back into the plan He had for me. God created other opportunities for me to establish relationships with the women in my community. He gave me a second chance, not because I owe Him but because He loves me.

God doesn't demand anything from us. He doesn't think we owe Him anything and He certainly doesn't expect us to fix ourselves before we encounter Him. He just patiently invites us to go for a walk with Him. He extends His hand of relationship and in that relationship we find wholeness. He does all this, not because of who we are, what we've done or because we are indebted to Him. He rescues and restores us because of who He is, because of

His all-encompassing love and divine Father's heart. He does it because that's who He is and who He is loves us.

How magnificent is that?

Chapter *Twelve*

HEARTBROKEN

Ezekiel 36:26 & 27

I will give you a new heart and put a new spirit within you; I will take the heart of stone out of your flesh and give you a heart of flesh. I will put My Spirit within you and cause you to walk in My statute and you will keep My judgments and do them.

Pouty. Whiney. Cry-baby. Tattle-tale. Those are just some of the words that chased me through my childhood. I was a sensitive kid and I often got my feelings hurt. I cried easily and sulking was a natural expression for me. My cousins teased me relentlessly about being pouty and kids at school would count down until I cried after even the most minor incident or offence. I hated myself for every tear I shed in their presence, for every piece of ammunition I gave to them. I was ashamed of my weakness and my sensitivity but as hard as I tried I could never seem to get control.

Sometime during my early teen years I finally got a grip on my emotions – a stranglehold, really. I became skilled in the art of stuffing my emotions and masking my true feelings. I was careful not to laugh too loud, love too much or care too deeply. I avoided being hugged or touched and I never, ever cried, especially if there was even the slightest chance that someone might see. I prided myself on not being 'mushy' or 'soft' and I went to great lengths to protect this reputation. The by-product of this ridiculous obsession of being emotionless was that my heart developed a rock hard, impenetrable shell.

I grew used to my constrained heart and lived like this for years. I loved Mr. Awesome and The Wee Ones. I had friendships, I was part of my church and I loved my family. I loved and served God. I gave Jesus my whole heart; my whole, encrusted, contained heart. I thought I was loving true but choosing to toughen up cost me my ability to really feel, to be wholly in the moment, to be alive with love.

I'm not sure how long I would have carried on living with my rigid and controlled heart, maybe forever. Thankfully, God saved me from myself. Again. He saw an opportunity to step in and do a miracle in my life. He used a circumstance that could have crushed my spirit to break through the shell of my heart. He bombarded me with love until my tough heart was pummeled into a tender, feeling, beating organ of life. God used cancer to heal my heart.

I was 35 years old when I was diagnosed with breast cancer. It was aggressive; my tumor was huge and growing quickly. Without radical medical intervention the prognosis wasn't good. My life went from the predictable routine of a stay-at-home mom to a blurred series of doctors' appointments and intrusive medical procedures. Within six weeks of the diagnosis I underwent surgery and began a year of treatments to eradicate the cancer that had infiltrated my body.

That year could have been the worst year of my life. I could have filled my mind with thoughts of how unjust the situation was, how I was being robbed of my life and how this was a burden that Mr. Awesome and The Wee Ones should never have to carry. I could have railed against God and been angry that He would allow such a thing to happen to me. I could have but I didn't.

I did have my moments. At times it was all very surreal. I had a hard time wrapping my brain around the fact that I was a cancer patient, that this was really happening. There were moments during recovery, after my surgery in particular, that I laughed at how ridiculous this whole situation was. Although I viewed my situation with disbelief at times, I never lost my belief in God. I did not, for one second, believe that He did this to me or even allowed this disease to enter my body. I knew my God better than that. From the moment that the doctor said the word cancer God grabbed me, held me tight and whispered into my heart, "I've got this kid – hang on tight and see what I can do!"

The first thing He did was break my heart through kindness. Friends, neighbors, family members and strangers blessed us with meals, childcare and financial gifts to help ease the stress and strain that the appointments and treatments put on our time and budget. Every time we turned around someone was coming up with another creative yet practical way to extend kindness and meet a need in our life. Beyond the practical needs, all of these wonderful people cared for my soul, too. I did not go a week during that entire year of treatment without receiving a phone call, email, card or visit from someone who just wanted me to know that they were rooting for me and praying for me.

Each time someone stepped up with a word or act of love my stony heart would crack a little more. It was terrifying at first. I was afraid of falling apart. I knew that if I let these people with their casseroles and smiles past my tough exterior that would be the end of me. I was afraid of becoming a blubbering mess. I was afraid that if I started crying I wouldn't be able to stop. I was afraid of being weak just when I most needed to be strong.

I tried to pull back but people were relentless with their kindness and love and homemade soup. Everywhere I went people smiled, squeezed my hand and offered words of encouragement. Then people started hugging me. Like really hugging me. Not those awkward side hugs we inflict on each other in the church foyer, either, but serious chest-to-chest bear hugs. The kind of hugs where you can feel the hugger willing their very life force into the huggee. Those hugs broke my heart wide open.

The funny thing is, that when my heart broke, the thing that I had feared the most never happened. I didn't fall apart. I didn't lose control. I didn't become a sobbing wreck. The opposite occurred. When my heart of stone broke there was suddenly room for love. I could give and receive love freely. I could feel the love of My People, my friends, neighbors, family and strangers who had lent their strength and hope to me in my time of need. I could feel their love, and God's love, as a tangible presence in my life. My broken heart allowed God to put me back together.

God was faithful to His word to me in that season. He brought health back to my body and life to my heart. He revived my spirit and renewed my hope. He reminded me daily, through the people in my world, that He saw me, loved me and still had a great big life planned for me. Through every act of kindness, every word of encouragement He whispered to me that He wasn't finished with me yet.

My broken heart has been put back together. It has been tied together with strings of love and kindness. It beats strong and true for those whom I love. And for all that God loves, too. I feel. I cry. I laugh. Deeply, fully, madly. I am fully alive in every moment and loving it, really loving it. For the first time, I can completely relate with something Mother Teresa said. She was once quoted as saying, "May God break my heart so completely that the whole world falls in." For me, He did and I pray He continues to ... everyday.

THINKING US THROUGH

Jeremiah 29:11-13

*For I know the thoughts that I think toward you,
says the Lord, thoughts of peace and not of evil,
to give you a future and a hope. Then you will
call upon Me and go and pray to Me and I will
listen to you. And you will seek Me and find Me,
when You search for Me with all your heart.*

Bad things happen. It's horrible, unfair and heartbreaking.
Natural disasters, disease and calamities occur daily. Good people
lose out just as often as bad people and we, the witnesses to these
unjust tragedies, shake our fists at God and demand to know why
He would allow such devastation to happen. We question whether
He really is a loving God when the world is full of such senseless
destruction and overwhelming loss.

In an effort to comfort each other we say things like, "what
doesn't kill you, makes you stronger" and "God never gives

you more than you can handle" but those are empty words that offer no help and little comfort. They reinforce the idea that God, somehow, enjoys seeing His children suffer and struggle; that He imagines ways to put them to the test to see just how much they can take. We forget that we have a part to play in our own lives and those things that happened generations before we were born impact us still.

Of course I'm talking about Adam and Eve and their decision to walk away from the instructions God gave them and to chart their own course. In that one decision, they changed the rules for all time. They gave away the authority that God had entrusted to them. God gave them dominion over the earth and in their one act of disobedience they turned all that power over to the devil. They invited him into their world and allowed him to roam free and wreak havoc. They invited him into our world. From that moment to this we have lived with the consequence of disobedience and the decision to sin.

I have heard many people ask the question," if Adam and Eve disobeyed why do I have to suffer? I wouldn't make the same mistake they did." Oh, wouldn't you? You wouldn't disobey? You wouldn't sin? Every time we lie, cheat, gossip or hate we bite the apple again. Every time we don't do what we know we should do or do what we know we shouldn't do we commit the same wrong that Adam and Eve did thousands of years ago. Every time we behave contrary to what God requires of us, we invite the same consequences into our world that Adam and Eve invited into theirs.

So, with this understanding, is it all God's fault? Is the chaos, death and destruction we see in our world all committed by a vengeful God or is it possible that there is something else happening here? Is it possible that we bear some of the responsibility for the world we live in?

I had a hard time reconciling verses like Jeremiah 29:11 and what I've always been taught about a loving God with the horrible things that happen in the world and the heartbreak I've experienced in my own life. That is, until I understood this truth; the devil sits around thinking of how to get us into trouble but God thinks of ways to get us out of trouble. The devil corrupts hearts, leaves trails of temptation and opens doors of sin. His sole goal is to keep us as far away from our loving Father as he can. It's up to us to decide whether or not we are going to fall for his lies and choose the path of destruction he lays out.

There are things that happen in life that we don't choose, things that happen because sin is in the world. Things we have absolutely no control over. We don't choose to get cancer, to lose a child or for a natural disaster to wipe out all we've worked for. We don't choose these things but we do choose how we respond to them. We choose how we see God through our circumstances.

When we step back from our own shock and disappointment over what has happened and look at the big picture we will see that God is still there. In the midst of the worst tragedies and devastation there is still goodness, love and comfort to be found. We see it in acts of kindness and heroics. We see it in the generous spirit of one person to another. It is the power of Holy Spirit working through the hearts of men and women, stirring them to good works. This is the best evidence of a loving God at work in our lives.

God never leaves us alone. He never blames us for the messes we get ourselves into. He never sits back and leaves us to sort things out on our own. He is always there, providing a way through our circumstances. He specializes in loving us through our chaos and clearing a way back to Him. His plan, from the beginning of time, has always been to get us through the messes we step into so we can walk in relationship with Him. In our very worst moments, He is always thinking the very best for us because that's what loving fathers do.

Mr. Awesome is a great dad. When we discovered that I was pregnant with our first child he was ecstatic. In the instant he realized that Us Two were going to become We Three he began planning and preparing. He worked extra hours at his job so we could buy the things we needed for our baby. He heard that babies might be able to recognize voices while still in the womb so he spent hours talking, singing and reading to my stomach. He invested all this time with our baby, pre-birth; even though there was no guarantee our baby would recognize him.

He thought about life after the baby was born. He imagined early morning cuddles, play dates at the park, Christmas traditions and the first day of school. In that first moment of understanding that he was a father, a hundred years of hope wrapped around our baby. The baby was still so small, so weak, and so incapable of returning Mr. Awesome's love yet he still dreamed. The baby was not able to embrace Mr. Awesome but he allowed his thoughts to encircle our wee babe. The baby had not arrived yet but his father still hoped for his future. And that's nothing compared to how God thinks of us.

God's thoughts are greater than we could ever imagine and His capacity to love is infinite. He meditates on our loveliness. He dreams of our future. He replays, in His imagination, the moments we have spent with Him. He is in love with us. His love isn't dependent on circumstances. It isn't limited by our missteps and our misunderstanding of Him. We are weak, small and under developed. We haven't 'arrived' yet. And still God loves us. He dreams of us and He hopes for our future. He has a fluid plan for our lives based on His hope and love.

Our difficulties and doubt don't hurt God. He doesn't mind that we struggle to make sense out of the senseless just as long as we keep coming back to Him. He wants us to come to Him with our questions. He wants to be The One to walk us through our confusion. He wants us to come to Him for the answers because He has them. He has the truth. He is the truth. He is our Father, we are His children and He is here for us. Always.

Then you will call upon Me and go and pray to Me and I will listen to you.

Chapter *Fourteen*

BEAUTIFUL SURRENDER

Luke 22:41-43

And He was withdrawn from them about a stone's throw, and He knelt down and prayed, saying, "Father, if it be Your will, take this cup away from Me; nevertheless not My will, but Yours, be done." Then an angel appeared to Him from heaven, strengthening Him.

Hello. My name is Nichole and I'm a recovering control freak.

Seriously, if I had to name one area of my life that I feel God is constantly working on it would be this, my compulsive, consuming need to be the one in charge. Or self control. Or controlling my words. Or controlling my temper. Okay, clearly, the root issue is control, after all. I could say that I come by it honestly, as most of my maternal family suffers from the same affliction, but that's just an excuse. The truth is, I'm a control freak because I'm fearful, proud and selfish.

My control freak tendencies have been the loud, obnoxious elephant in the room through most of my married life, and probably for most of my natural life, if I'm being honest. The first real wake-up call to my own nature came when Crafty was just a year old. I suffered a back injury that left me completely unable to care for her, three-year-old Dude or myself. So, Mr. Awesome took the time off work to care for all of us. He cooked, cleaned, laundered and house-wifed like nobody's business. He really was amazing but I still felt the need to be an armchair quarterback or a couch-ridden nagging wife.

One day, when I was just getting some mobility back, friends stopped by for a visit. Mr. Awesome had done a load of laundry and was folding an array of tiny girl clothes, frilly bibs and odd shaped receiving blankets with much awkward determination. After watching him muddling through for a minute or two, while laying flat on my back unable to move without pain, I told him to hand the blankets to me and *I* would fold them properly because *he* was doing it wrong.

"You mean, he's not folding them your way," my friend said, laughing at me. " Just because he's not doing it your way doesn't mean he's doing it wrong."

Shocking as it might be, that is the first time I can remember thinking that maybe my way may not be the only way to do something – but it wasn't the last time I had this epiphany. This was the beginning of my own understanding that being a control freak was a serious roadblock in all of my relationships, that my desire to be in control was sending my life out of control. God, with His infinite patience and grace, has been working in my heart in this area for years and finally, I think He's making some inroads!

During a recent read through the Gospel of Luke I examined, with fresh eyes and an open heart, the passage about Jesus praying in the garden of Gethsemane. I saw something there that I can't remember ever reading before. Jesus was feeling the weight of all that was about to occur pressing in on Him. He knew that He was just moments from being betrayed, beaten and crucified. Although He is God, He is also a man and the full understanding of the physical pain and spiritual separation He was about to experience was upon Him. He was afraid and He was struggling so He prayed. Jesus took all His fear and uncertainty to God in prayer.

"Not My will, but Yours, be done."

There on His knees, Jesus surrendered His will to that of the Father. He trusted God, the Master of the Plan, to see Him through. Trust and surrender. God heard Him and answered Him. The thing is, God did not bend His will to Jesus' and Jesus didn't whine and complain. God stayed the course and Jesus followed. Jesus obeyed and God sent help and comfort to Jesus. Yes, you read that right. Jesus needed help and God sent it. This is what I had missed before but here it is:

Then an angel appeared from Heaven, strengthening Him.

Jesus cried out to God. He even offered a suggestion on how God might help Him and although God didn't, and couldn't, take the 'cup' from Him, He did hear the cries of His Son and respond. God didn't leave Jesus alone in His pain and fear. He sent someone to strengthen Him. He sent someone to be with Him. The circumstances didn't change. God didn't remove the pressure but He did provide help. God didn't leave Him alone in His moment of need; God, the Father, didn't disappoint Him.

Humans are funny beings. We say we trust God, we say He is our Provider and Protector. We say we turn all our troubles over to Him but only until our troubles become too big or until we disagree with His handling of our troubles, as if we could do better on our own. The moment our worries become greater than our understanding of God we snatch back all that we had surrendered.

"Here God, I give you my illness, my rocky relationship, my rebellious teen, my empty bank account," we say and then our illness turns out to be cancer, infidelity enters our already rocky relationship, the teen rebellion is actually an eating disorder and the empty bank account has led to phone calls from creditors. It all piles up and we panic. We grab our issues back from God. Our worry overshadows our surrender and we pull our mess back into our own laps because what? We can do better than God? We are better problem solvers and mess managers than He is?

For me, most of my controlling tendencies are used as a safeguard against disappointment. I think that if I control the situation and things don't work out then I have no one to blame but myself. I won't be disappointed or let down by anyone – ever – if I stay in control. I won't ever be angry with anyone, not my friends, not my family, not God, if I stay in control. I mask my fear of being let down with pride and that leads me to behave selfishly and over the years this has wreaked havoc in my life.

Being a control freak has strangled the life out of my relationships, it has limited God's ability to work in and through my life and it has cost me my peace and joy on more occasions than I can remember. My fight to keep control has left me hollow, angry and alone ... not the life I really want for myself.

Thankfully, God is patient and so is Mr. Awesome. God has used Mr. Awesome's natural goodness and gentleness to teach me what it really means to trust without limitations and that being disappointed by someone is rarely fatal. Together they have accepted me as I am and loved me into a trust relationship and gradually I am relinquishing my death grip on things that are really beyond my control anyway.

Day by day, I am realizing that if I follow Jesus' example, if I come to God in prayer and surrender all to His capable hands and allow Him to strengthen me then all will truly be well. One step at a time, one circumstance at a time, I am learning to trust. I am learning that God can handle my disappointment and if I hang in there my disappointment will turn to awe at all that God can and will do. When I truly and wholly surrender to Him, when I whisper those powerful words, "not my will but Yours," I open the door to His unstoppable grace and love.

Not my will but yours. Always. Forever.

Chapter

HIS COMPASSIONATE HEART

John 11:35

Jesus wept

I grew up attending Sunday school. I loved the Bible stories and puppet skits and the crafts and games but the thing I loved most of all about my Sunday school was the competitions. Each month my teacher would announce a different competition and I would do my best to win one of the Bible comic books or bookmarks he offered as a prize. I had a good shot at the prize on Bring Your Bible month and Friendship month but I was hooped when it was Good Listener month (aka Don't Talk During the Lesson month). My favorite, though, was Scripture Memory month because I had an excellent memory. I knew all the best verses to memorize and I racked up the points with gems like John 11:35. Easy, peasy. Just two words. *Jesus wept,* big deal. Give me my points and let's move on.

I remember coming across this verse again when I was a teen and I thought the whole thing was a little weird. Jesus cried. I mean, really, He was the Savior of the world. He was God; what does God have to cry over? If He didn't like something He could change it. Besides, in this instance, Jesus was crying over a dead guy who he knew wasn't going to stay dead. The other thing that bothered me was that Jesus' pal, the guy writing this account of His life, John the Beloved, outed the weepy Christ. I mean, seriously, you'd think a friend would have His back!

It wasn't until recently that I understood why this moment, these tears were so significant. It wasn't until I read this story again and viewed it through the eyes of my own disappointment and heartache that I understood why Jesus wept as He did. It wasn't until I cried my own tears, while believing in God's goodness, that I became whole-heartedly thankful for this shameless display of love and compassion from my Jesus.

The story is this: Jesus had just arrived at the home of His dear friends, Mary, Martha and Lazarus to find Lazarus dead. He had been in a nearby town, ministering, when He received word that Lazarus was unwell. Still, knowing how sick His friend was, Jesus completed His time of ministry before He made His way to Lazarus' house. He knew that Lazarus was going to be dead by the time He arrived but He also knew that Lazarus' death wouldn't be fatal.

As Jesus approached the house, He took in the scene. Mary was mourning and wailing with her mourning and wailing friends, Martha was busy covering her grief with the practical day-to-day business of managing a death and Lazarus was, most decidedly, dead. Jesus stood in the midst of the sorrow and heartbreak of His friends and wept. Even knowing that Lazarus was about to live again, Jesus wept.

Why would Jesus bother with the tears when He was moments away from creating a moment of intense celebration? Why get caught up in the temporary emotion of grief when life was right around the corner? Because Jesus loved. Jesus loved the heartbroken Mary, the emotionally stunted Martha and the very dead Lazarus. These were His people, His heart was connected to their hearts and their hearts were aching. And so was His.

Shortly after Mischief's second birthday, Mr. Awesome and I began thinking about adding to our family. If these three kids were this cute and amazing, just imagine what a fourth would be like! With reasoning like that, it didn't take us long to make the decision to expand us five to an even six. In January of 2007 we became pregnant with our fourth child.

From the instant the pregnancy test showed a little plus sign my imagination leapt into full gear. I started dreaming and planning for this much-wanted little princess. Oh yes, I was sure that I was having a girl. I imagined her sweet freckled nose and delicate baby features. I daydreamed about the toddler she would become and the little girl she would grow into. I visualized Christmas mornings, summer vacations and first days of school with my four children.

All of these plans and dreams came to a screeching halt when I started experiencing complications with my pregnancy in the beginning of March. Despite bed rest and weekly ultrasounds to track the progress of my sweet baby girl the complications persisted and my worst fears became my reality. On March 30 my baby's heart stopped beating. My baby, my lovely little Jessie Joy, had died.

I wept.

I was devastated, heartbroken and completely undone. I couldn't believe that *this* was happening to *me*. I had three normal, healthy pregnancies and gave birth to three normal, healthy kids. We were good parents. We wanted our kids. We loved our kids. We loved Jesus. Why was this happening? Why was this happening to me?

That night, the night we knew we had lost Jessie, I cried myself to sleep. My last conscious thought was, 'I didn't get to hold her and I don't even have a picture to remember her by.' When I awoke hours later Mr. Awesome was sitting beside the bed, holding my hand. He leaned over, kissed my forehead and asked if I had dreamt of anything while I slept. I was irritated that he would ask such a stupid question at a time like that and was prepared to snap at him, when I remembered that I had dreamt.

I dreamed that I was standing at an open window with a blank canvas set up on an easel beside me. As I looked out the window, I was momentarily blinded by a warm, white light that shone as if it were the sun but wasn't. When my eyes adjusted to the brightness I saw a lush, flower-filled meadow in front of me. The meadow was also full of children, so many children running, laughing and playing with each other but not so many that I couldn't see her; a little girl with golden brown hair that glistened in the light. She was wearing a white dress with a red sash and she was spinning and dancing all by herself. I recognized her immediately because she belonged to me. That little girl was my girl. My Jessie Joy. And she was safe and happy and perfect there in the meadow.

I believe that God gave me that vision of my daughter, safe in His care, to help heal my broken heart. He gave me a picture to carry in my heart to comfort me because He loves me. And because He loves me, my sorrow became His. He had compassion for me – just as Jesus did for His friends Mary and Martha.

It turns out that Jesus' pal, John the Beloved, did have His back after all. And he had ours too. He recorded this moment so that we, thousands of years after this incident, would know that Jesus holds us in His very heartbeat. John saw Jesus' tears as part of the thread that connects us to our Friend, our Savior.

Knowing that Jesus is with me in my sorrow as much as He is with me in my joy brings me comfort. I feel a sense of relief knowing that my tears don't annoy Him and there is no heavenly, "Get over it!" waiting for me. Jesus is with me in my moment of grief but I don't stay there. He steps into my grief, my heartache, my sorrow to take me by the hand and guide me through all of that devastation and into my time of life, joy and celebration.

Accepting God's comfort and compassion doesn't erase the significance of the loss, it just eases the weight of it. I still miss my Jessie Joy and her brother Alex William whom we lost later that same year. But I know they are there, in that meadow, waiting for me. Until then, they are safe is Jesus' care and so am I.

Chapter *Sixteen*

ALL I NEED

Hebrews 13:5

*Let your conduct be without covetousness;
be content with such things as you have. For
He Himself said, "I will never leave you or
forsake you."*

Am I enough?

That was the question that resonated through my spirit when I
read this verse. I was feeling particularly low and kind of pouting
to God about how unfair things were. I volunteered my time and
resources to our church. I led a women's Bible study and coor-
dinated our children's program. Every week I interacted with
dozens of people in our church and community but here I was
alone again. I was throwing a pity party and I was the guest of
honor, in fact, I was the only guest.

I had been on a social media site earlier in the evening and saw
pictures of several of my friends from Bible study out together at

a local restaurant for appetizers. And another friend had updated her status, naming a number of friends from our community who were at her place for a girls' night. A bunch of my cousins had gathered earlier in the week but no one thought to invite me. My birthday had just passed with very little mention from any of my friends. I felt slighted, left out and ignored.

It had been a rough couple of months for me. Truth be told, the last couple of years had been relationally rocky. We had moved away from our hometown and had established ourselves in a new church and community. I was happy with our move and I knew it was the very thing that God had planned for us. But growing new friendships wasn't as easy as I had hoped it would be. I have a fairly high D.Q., Dork Quotient. I have a hard time being at ease with new people and I'm constantly worried about dorking out on them. And then there was that other thing, the relatively new thing that made it even more difficult for me to relate to others.

There's no real name for it and I struggle to find a way to describe it that doesn't make me sound like a total wingnut. God found me when I was four years old but I didn't really find Him, and fully awaken to all the possibilities a life *in* Him brings, until a couple of years ago. But when I did, everything changed for me. It was like waking up with a new super power that I had no idea of how to manage.

I was raised in a loving, Godly home. I attended a private Christian school, Sunday school and Youth Group all through my growing up years. I volunteered in church and spent time reading my Bible. When I became a mother I set about teaching my children as I had been taught. I did all the right things and I loved God with my whole heart but still I felt like something was missing. Like I was somehow one step out of sync with where I should be.

There was no one incident that triggered it; it was more of a gradual awakening, a slow understanding of the pieces I was missing. Day by day, I surrendered my limited understanding of who God was, and what He was capable of, and opened my heart to all the possibilities of life in Him. I began to understand my purpose, His love and The Church Body in a deeper way. With this new understanding came an absolute confidence in His faithfulness and active presence in my life. And that changed me – drastically, in some ways.

I believe there are seasons of life when God is working so intensely on us that He requires our full attention. When we open our hearts to Him and say, "Use me, shape me, mold me." He will but it will be painful and wonderful and radical. He will peel away rough and damaged parts, expose our deepest wounds and heal them. He will light a fire in our hearts and apply pressure from the outside so that the very shape of our nature is changed. He will redefine possible and fill us with wild dreams. That's what happened to me. I found God, He found me and all was changed.

I didn't manage this change very gracefully, though, and some of my friends didn't know what to make of me anymore. I had a difficult time talking about surface, what I deemed as frivolous, things when God was working so deeply in my life. I hungered for the things of God so fully that anything - any movie, song or conversation - that was not of Him irritated me, like sand in a wet bathing suit. And, I'm afraid my irritation and disinterest showed.

Looking back, I can see now where I should have been more patient, more accepting and more loving. I can also see where some other choices I made and friendships I pruned were exactly right. But even in that, I could have been more gentle in those situations.

At any rate, as I emerged from this season, I felt lonely and out of sync with most of the people around me. I would see groups of people enjoying each other and I would be envious. I would hear of gatherings after the fact and I would feel hurt and left out. People I didn't particularly want to hang with anymore would talk about going to places and doing things that held no interest to me and I would still sulk. It was during one of those pouting bouts that God asked me The Question. *Am I enough?*

I had just come through this beautiful season of being With God. I felt His presence working in and through me. I felt closer to Him than I had ever before in my life. I had grown and matured spiritually but as soon as I lifted my head and looked around I began to whine. I blamed God for my isolation instead of thanking Him for all that He had done in my life. So when I complained, He challenged me. Was it true? Were the words I sang, prayed and spoke true to my heart? Was God really enough? If the only friend I ever had was Him, would that be enough for me?

It took me some time to puzzle through this. The immediate answer was, 'yes!' but I had a sense that He wasn't looking for the right churchy answer. He wanted the answer that was true to my heart. If God, my Father, my Protector, my Provider, My Healer, my Everything was the only source of comfort, joy, peace and friendship I ever had would that be enough? Would it be enough to know that my Friend would never leave me or forsake me?

I eventually got to the place where my heart was full in Him and I could answer, "yes" truthfully. My envy and hurt diminished and I felt secure in the friendship I had in Christ. I still felt pangs of sadness when I wasn't included in parties and activities and it still hurt my feelings to be overlooked, but I was no longer devastated or overwhelmed with loneliness. And in this, just as with every other area of my life I surrendered, God, my Friend, proved faithful.

Almost as soon as I relinquished my right to have hurt feelings over friendships He introduced me to a whole group of wonderful, life-giving friends. Some were new friends, others were acquaintances who attended church with me each week but whom I had never really connected with before. Still others were old friends I had lost touch with. Each new connection, or reconnection, humbled me and filled me with thankfulness because, even in this, He did not forsake me.

I am thankful for my friends. They bring encouragement, joy and fun to my life. They challenge me to grow in God and support me in times of trial. I love my friends, my God-family, My People. But I rely on God. He is still all I need.

Section

Three

One Big Messy Family

The morning after I came home from the hospital with wee (okay, not so wee ... he was over ten pounds!) baby Dude Mr. Awesome and I stayed in bed with our little miracle for hours. We oohed and aahed, we studied his teeny thumb nails and his wrinkly toes, we stroked his peach fuzz and watched his beautiful face while he slept. We were utterly enraptured by this tiny human we made and we seriously considered staying cocooned away in our bed forever.

We didn't want the loud, crazy, and messy outside world to spoil our bubble of happiness but we knew that eventually all that was Out There would affect all that was In Here. Soon our home was flooded with aunts, uncles, cousins, grandparents, neighbors and friends. Everyone wanted to have a look at the human we made. Everyone wanted to hold him and nuzzle him. Everyone wanted to give their opinion on who he looked like and how I should care for him. Everyone wanted in on this moment, and frankly, it was exhausting, frustrating, discouraging and bubble bursting. It was also wonderful.

Family is messy. You've got the aunt who always says the wrong thing at the wrong time, the uncle who complains about everything, the cousin who always gets her way and the great-aunt's loopy second husband who really should not be allowed out in public anymore for all the inappropriate comments and gestures. But these are your people. The aunt who brings you meals when you're sick and never forgets your birthday. The uncle who would drop everything at a moment's notice to help you out of a jam. The cousin who shares all your secret childhood memories and is always rooting for you. And that great-aunt's second husband who loves you like you are his own kid and believes you can do anything. These are your messy, exhausting, lovely, wonderful people and you wouldn't trade them for anything.

That's church. Church is a crazy place. It's a great big family gathering with all the nuts and flakes. It's a chaotic jumble of people who love each other because they love God, and more importantly, He loves them. It's a group of strangers bound together in the promise of eternity. It's iron sharpening iron. It's mentorship. It's friendship. It's imperfect love offered in the most perfect way. It's family.

Our relationship with God is meant to be personal but not private. It is meant to be worked out between us and our Heavenly Father, in the safety of community. We can never fully understand the depth and intensity of God's love until we love others and allow others to love us. And yes, this will be horribly messy and terribly wonderful, all in the same moment. That's church. That's family. That's how it's meant to be.

Chapter Seventeen

LIVE GRACE

Ephesians 4:32

And be kind to one another, tender hearted, forgiving one another, even as God in Christ forgave you.

Grace is a hefty concept to understand. It often seems illusive, yet it's such a vital piece, perhaps the most vital piece, of our love story with God. Without grace we would still be lost, alone and without relationship. We would still be trying to earn our way into some kind of friendship with God, a task that is beyond our capabilities. It is understanding the grace we receive that allows us to pass grace along to those in our world and maybe that's where our problem begins.

It's our human nature to desire justice, to see the playing field balanced and to see those who cause suffering to suffer. There's a piece of our nature - more prominent in some than others - that loves seeing people pay for their nastiness. I'm not talking about our desire to see criminals pay for their crimes, I'm talking about that sweet moment when the liar gets caught in a lie or the cheater is double crossed or the gossip gets stung by their own words. Those moments of relational justice seem so satisfying in the moment but the satisfaction rarely lasts. Justice doesn't heal our wounds. Grace does.

I have been deeply hurt by people. I have been gossiped about, used and betrayed. In the moment of my hurt, I would have loved to see these people get what was coming to them, I would have loved to see them pay for what they did to me, but once the moment had passed my greatest wish was for a heartfelt apology. More often than not I didn't get the apology I was hoping for but in every case they got exactly what they deserved. God's unending grace.

And so did I.

God loved us when we were undeserving. He chose us when we rejected Him. He sought us when we hid from Him. He rescued us before we ever knew we were lost. He forgave us before we were ever sorry. He forgave us even knowing that some of us would never come to Him and ask for forgiveness. That's grace. His unending divine protection and love, freely given. No strings attached. No conditions. No fine print. Grace is there. For the taking. For all of us. Whether we deserve it or not.

This has been a long and difficult lesson to learn. I have a strong sense of justice, especially when it comes to me and mine. But I have seen, time and again, the benefits of extending grace to others especially when it's not asked for, or, in my opinion, deserved. Grace brings relationship, healing and affection. Grace builds family and binds friends together. Grace is what makes us divine in our humanity.

Just as we began to make sense of this idea of grace for ourselves as a family, a real-life opportunity to live grace, and teach grace to our kids, walked through our front door. Dude had been having a rough year at school and a few kids in particular had been making him a target of their aggression and the butt of their jokes. They had used his quirks and challenges for their entertainment but after several meetings with the school, Dude and one of the boys sat down and began to work things out. They decided to give friendship a try and we were thrilled.

We invited this boy, Champ, into our home in hopes of helping these guys transition from enemies to friends. We knew that Champ had had some lows in his life that had left him wary of trusting people and that he had a tendency of lashing out at people who got close to him. But we could see it was a defensive maneuver he used to ensure that he was always the one leaving and never again the one being left. We soon discovered that most of his unfriendly behavior at school was a result of trying to fit in with someone, anyone. He really was a pretty neat kid, once we got to know him. He was funny, creative and sensitive. Loving this kid was easy, just not simple.

Unfortunately, true to his pattern, Champ eventually fell back into his old crowd of friends, made up mostly of kids who liked to torment and humiliate Dude. We were all sad to see this but we continued to be kind and inviting to Champ whenever we saw him at school or in the community. Things continued this way for quite a while, until Champ used the confidence he had gained with Dude to betray and demean him in front of a group of kids in the school library.

That day, Dude got into the van after school and burst into tears. He was angry, confused and embarrassed. He felt like a fool for trusting Champ and hated him for 'weaseling' his way into his friendship. Dude explained the whole humiliating scene. I was heartsick for my boy. Instant anger against Champ tried to well up within me, but it fizzled out. I could only feel sadness for Champ. And forgiveness.

Dude's path to forgiveness was a little longer and had a few more turns. He understood that walking around with a heart full of hate was keeping him from enjoying life. He could see how he was missing out on other friendships and great opportunities because he was trapped in his own anger. He realized that Champ and the other boys had moved on as if nothing had happened but he was still stuck in the moment of betrayal.

"If he'd only say he was sorry then I'd forgive him!" Dude lamented one night. It had been about a week since the library incident and Dude was missing his buddy. He had come to the place where he knew, if Champ asked, he could forgive him and they could be friends again. I explained, as best I could, that he needed to forgive Champ even if he never, ever apologized for what he had said. He needed to set his own heart free and understand that grace is given, not deserved.

I'm not sure when or how it happened but God and Dude worked things out and eventually Dude was able to forgive Champ. I don't know whether Champ has ever apologized for this incident but I am sure both boys have learned the value of forgiving and being forgiven. I have seen both Dude and Champ give and receive grace many times on their way back into friendship. And I am so proud of them for learning something at the age of thirteen that it took me many more years to wrap my head around.

Through my own life experiences, on both sides of the offence, I've come to learn that true forgiveness is not dependent on being asked for it. It can't be. If we only forgive when people ask for it, when they step forward and admit that they were wrong, then the forgiveness isn't about God's goodness, it is about yours. You make forgiveness a gift from you not a transfer of grace from the Father.

Whenever we have a conversation about grace and forgiveness in our house we always come back to the same sentence. *Because we are forgiven we can pass the grace we so freely enjoy on to others.* It's become part of who we are, who we are teaching our kids to be. It's our motto, our standard, our antidote for bitterness and judgment. It is the truth that we live because of God's generosity. It's the reminder of the freedom we have because God gave before we asked.

God created us to be in community with Him and with one another. We can't live that part of our design without grace. We first need to accept God's grace, His unending, limitless love and forgiveness for us and then we must do our best to extend that same grace to others. We need to forgive before it's asked for and love through unloveliness. We need to love like Christ and live grace. Freely.

Chapter *Eighteen*

GRACE GROWERS

Matthew 5:43-45

*You have heard that it was said, "You shall love
your neighbor and hate your enemy." But I say
to you, love your enemies, bless those who curse
you, do good to those who hate you and pray for
those who spitefully use you and persecute you,
that you may be sons of your Father in heaven;
for He makes the sun rise on the evil and on the
good and sends rain on the just and on the unjust.*

"Pray for her."
"No thank you."
"Pray for her."
"Nope."
"Pray for her."
"I'll pray for her husband and kids; they need
it."
"Pray for her."
"I don't want to."
"Pray for her."

That's the gist of a conversation I had with Holy Spirit a number
of years ago. I was working on a project and one of the other team
members was a real treat to work with. She drove me nuts on a
daily basis and I did my best to avoid her. I would give myself pep
talks before I went to work and I would count down the minutes
until I could get away from her at the end of the day. Everything
about how she spoke and interacted with the team grated on me.
She was contrary, whiney, demanding, selfish and rude – and
those were her best qualities!

I only made it a few weeks into the project before I was ready
to quit. It took everything in me to keep control and not tell
her off whenever we were together. I stopped offering opinions
and contributing to the process, because it was just easier, but
my irritation level was through the roof. I spent way too much
time playing out different shaming scenarios in my head, what I
would say and what I would do to put her in her place if ever the
opportunity presented itself. It got to the point that I knew I had to
leave the team before I said or did something that would involve
mandatory hours of community service and possible anger man-
agement counseling to make amends for.

I made my decision to quit and went into the office to let the
supervisor know. I hadn't prayed about this decision and I hadn't
looked for alternative solutions. I just looked for the quickest and
easiest way out. As I was standing outside the supervisor's office,
waiting to see him, I had this conversation with God. Truth be
told, I was doing my best to ignore God but He was relentless. I
didn't end up quitting that day but I didn't start praying for her
either. I didn't think she needed prayer. I prayed for the poor
souls who had to live and work with her instead. I was sure they
needed it!

I continued to pray for the people around her for a number
of weeks and somewhere along the way my prayers started to
include her. It sort of happened by accident one day that I asked
God to bless her and thought, "what the heck, I might as well

include her, too." Not the most spiritual approach to obedience but it got me to where I was supposed to be all along. It wasn't long before I found myself praying for her often and at random times. I would be going about my normal life and suddenly she'd pop into my mind so I prayed. The more I prayed for her, the less annoying she became. The more I prayed for her the more I understood her. I actually came to like her!

I started volunteering to work with her on different elements of the project. I invited her out for coffee after work and spent time getting to know her, all the while still praying for her. I began to see her quirks and personality idiosyncrasies in a different light. She wasn't contrary and whiney; she was worried about failing. She wasn't demanding and rude; she was a straightforward communicator. She wasn't selfish; she was insecure. I also learned that she was creative, generous and fiercely loyal.

So what happened? Did my prayers change her? No, my prayers changed me. God took my judgmental, irritated heart and softened it. He used my time in prayer to reshape my perspective and humble me. He opened my eyes so that I could see her how He sees her. Precious, valuable and lovely.

It's easy to love those who are gentle, kind and generous. It's a cakewalk to serve the popular, beautiful, connected people in your world. It's a pleasure to bless the talented, lovely and powerful people you know. Anyone can inconvenience themselves for those people but what about the demanding, selfish, ornery, contentious people? Can you serve those people just as joyfully? Can you extend the same measure of love to those who seemingly make every effort to be unlovable?

Jesus knew that this was going to be one of the biggest challenges of our lives but He had also seen the damage unloving hearts were capable of doing to each other. Through the generations those who indulged in feelings of hate and revenge tore apart families and communities. They completely missed God's best for their lives because they were too busy focusing on the worst in each other. Jesus doesn't want that for us. So He gives us the key to loving those who push us to our limits. He reminds us whose we are.

... and pray for those who spitefully use you and persecute you, that you may be sons of your Father in heaven.

We are God's kids so we are to love as He loves. We are the children of the Most High God so we must rise to His standard. Jesus points out that even the most despicable person can love the lovely but our ability to love those who make it difficult to love them, those who hate us, use us and treat us badly, our ability to love them is what sets us apart as the children of God. His unconditional, boundless love flowing through us is the evidence of His greatness at work in our lives.

I'm not really a people person. I have a natural bent toward sarcasm and cynicism and a low tolerance for stupidity that make loving a learned trait. I have had to work hard to learn to love as Jesus loves, to see people as He sees them. Even with all my efforts to learn to love better, often my first instinct is to be annoyed with people, to judge too harshly and look for the nearest escape route out of these cumbersome relationships. I have a friend who calls these relationships 'grace growers.' She encourages me to look at these people, and all their annoying traits, as opportunities to grow beyond myself. I know she's right ... and that annoys me!

Seriously though, somewhere along the journey of praying for others I had an IGIM. Forever is a long time to spend with someone who annoys me. I'd be far better off learning to love them on this side of eternity than waiting for a heavenly scolding for all the time I've wasted being irritated when I could have been in community with them instead. The bottom line is, if your grace grower is a believer, you're family. You will be with them forever so why not pray now and love now? After all, someone somewhere is praying to love you ... and me!

I know that I am someone's grace grower (probably several people's) and if they are taking the time to pray for me, to see me as God sees me, to love me despite my unloveliness, shouldn't I at least attempt to do the same for someone else? Jesus only made two commandments during His time on earth. One is to love God, the other is to love people. It must be really important to Him that we love each other and if it's that important to Him it should be just as important to us. Pray and love, pray and love.

Chapter Nineteen

LOVE IS THE THING

1 Corinthians 12:31 – 13:3

But earnestly desire the best gifts. And yet I show you a more excellent way. Though I speak with the tongues of men and of angels but have not love, I have become sounding brass or a clanging symbol. And though I have the gift of prophecy and understand all mysteries and all knowledge and though I have all faith so that I could remove mountains, but have not love, I am nothing. And though I bestow all my goods to feed the poor, and though I give my body to be burned but have not love, it profits me nothing.

I love gifts. I love seeing neatly wrapped packages on Christmas morning or odd-shaped works of art on Mother's Day. My heart skips a beat at spying a hand-written note in my mailbox and I am flooded with joy when a friend delivers a much-needed coffee.

More than the gift, though, it's the thought behind it that touches my heart. I get the warm and fuzzies at the thought of someone thinking about me. A gift given with love is the sweetest thing.

The apostle Paul knew that. He knew the secret to This Great Adventure was, and is, love. He knew that above doctrine, theology, spiritual gifts, titles and position is love. Love is where it all began. Because of love Jesus took our place on the cross and paid the debt for our sin. Because of love He rose again to prepare a place for us in Heaven so that we could spend eternity with Him. Because of love we have the privilege of being in relationship with Him, right now.

But sometimes we silly, fickle humans forget about love. We lose the plot and focus on gifts, positions and titles. We spend our time and efforts chasing temporary rewards of good service and seeking accolades. We get busy doing good, doing church, doing life. We become consumed with the appearance of holiness and forget that love is the goal. Love is the thing. Love is where it begins and ends. Love, not piety, religion or charity. Not even holiness alone can trump love. We fail to realize that we can't be holy without love because God is the standard of holiness and He is the embodiment of love. The two cannot be separated. Holiness can only be attained through love.

Paul knew it. Paul lived it. Before he was Paul, pastor at large, he was Saul, religious Christian hunter. He lived for the appearance of holiness but he did so out of religious obligation and not out of a love for God or His people. Everything Saul did was for status and show. He wanted to seem holy, to look like he was doing all the right things, without having to actually get his hands dirty with all that messy relational stuff. He wanted the status of holiness without the love relationship with God. That is, until he literally saw the light.

Saul had an encounter with Jesus. On his way to conduct the business of piety Paul came face to face with the very definition of holiness. Love grabbed him and in response he abandoned all, his title, his position and even his name. He left the pursuit of religious fame in favor of the quest for love; holy, righteous, pure God-love. For the proclamation of this God-love Saul, turned Paul, dedicated his life, sacrificed his comfort and forfeited his safety. He gave it all for the mission that was set before him.

Jesus asked Paul to grow and serve His church and so he did. Paul didn't commit to this out of a religious duty or in hopes of earning heavenly brownie points. He did it because he had a revelation of the depth of Jesus' love for him - a sinner, a murderer, a loveless wretch. Paul experienced first-hand the limitless, transformative power of a loving and lasting encounter with Jesus. He knew what he had been before Jesus and he saw what he had become after Jesus. The change was night and day and he was compelled to pass along his knowledge of the source of This Love.

When I read this passage of 1 Corinthians, I like to think about the image and life of Paul. I love the contrast and symmetry that is Paul's love affair with God and His people. To look at him, love may not have been the first word that came to mind. The accepted physical description of Paul is short, bald, bow-legged and heavily scarred. He had been beaten, ship wrecked, flogged, stoned and left for dead. His heart could have turned against God because of all that he had suffered for the name of Jesus but it didn't. He could have questioned God, railed against the unfairness of his situation and allowed bitterness to overtake him. But he didn't.

Paul, instead, opened his heart to love and let it fill him, protect him and compel him. He soaked in the truth of God's unending love for His children and he spread this truth wherever he went. He was anything but beautiful in his physical appearance but he was entirely lovely where it mattered most, his heart.

Paul allowed God to open his heart and fill it with the very thing that fills His own heart. Us. His people. His children. God's heart beats for us. He is madly, deeply, truly in love with us and it is His greatest desire for us to know Him, to be in relationship with Him. The idea of us with Him is what fills His heart and that's the very thing Paul allowed to fill him, to compel him into action. He allowed himself to be consumed with the passion to connect God's children to their Father. He lived this call, this passion in his everyday eating, working, breathing, loving life.

It can be so easy to go through the motions in our modern culture. We can sponsor a child from the other side of the world. We can buy a wristband to support a cause. We can watch a documentary about social injustice. All of these things make us feel informed, educated and as if we're participating in a solution. We can volunteer for an hour a week or an hour a month at our local church and feel like we've fulfilled our duty to love The Church. But is that enough? Is that all God really requires of us? Is the appearance of holiness the best we can do?

We can appear super spiritual and have an amazing talent. We can raise millions of dollars for great causes and we can volunteer hundreds of hours in our communities but what is it all worth if it's done out of duty? What's the point if we're missing love? If we don't give and serve from a heart full of love it's all for nothing. It's hollow and meaningless.

Jesus doesn't want our duty He wants our love. He doesn't want our money He wants our devotion. He doesn't want us to buy into a cause. He wants us to give Him our hearts. It's not enough to appear or to do. He wants us to be. Be The Church. Be the love.

Love first. Just love. Let everything you say, everything you are, flow out of your heart of love. Let the life you lead and the scars you bear in the name of Christ be the very image of love. Let love be the best gift you receive and the best gift you give. Let love be the driving force in your life, the thing that compels you, calls you and gives you a passion to be. Love is the thing.

Chapter *Twenty*

UNVEILED

2 Corinthians 3:18

*But we all, with unveiled face, beholding as in
a mirror the glory of the Lord, are being transformed into the same image from glory to glory,
just as by the Spirit of the Lord*

It is human nature to put our best image forward. The fashion and
beauty industries make millions of dollars every year by persuad-
ing people to carefully craft their image with the right brands.
They tell us that our clothes, cosmetics, accessories and hair
products send a message about the quality of person we are. The
labels we wear define us and shape our public persona.

What happens in The Church is not that much different than
what happens in the world. We spend hours, sometimes years,
crafting our image, honing our holiness. We balance our understanding of the accepted rules for modern Christianity with our
personal take on 'in the world, not of the world' relatability to

come up with our own style of Christianity. We market our own brand of Christianity based on the role that suits us best.

Some of us become the Uber Christian. We carry a Bible with us everywhere and we quote scripture in lieu of making real conversation. Others of us swing the opposite way and take on the role of the Edgy Christian, accessorizing our life with tattoos, piercings and an aloof Jesus-loves-me-and-I'm-cool-with-that attitude. Then there's the Buffet Christian who takes random verses and theologies that best suit the lifestyle they want to live and creates a smorgasbord approach to faith. Or maybe the Robo Christian is more your speed. You learn Christianese, complete with slang and trendy sayings, you trade all discernable personality for a holy demeanor and you embrace the idea of being a stranger and an alien in this world. Or maybe Sister Intercessor or Brother Prosperity or Deacon Judgment or the limited edition Super Volunteer Christian resonates better with you.

Whatever the image you choose, the goal is the same; hide as much of the unlovely as possible. For some reason, we feel like as soon as we give our lives to Christ we have to slap on a pair of spiritual Spanx to contain all our wobbly bits. We feel the need to appear like a Christian even before we understand what being a Christ follower really is. We tell ourselves that we have to look the part before we can enter into community and relationship. We then try to make ourselves presentable so that He can make us holy. But that's all backwards. We've got it all wrong.

What would happen if we stopped hiding who we really are and where we really come from and just got real with each other? Paul, in his second letter to the church in Corinth, encourages them to do just that. He reminds them that once God gets involved there is no reason to hide, in fact, we should do exactly the opposite. We should reveal the truth to each other so that we may reflect all that God has done to transform us. He encourages The Church to be honest about where they've come from so that everyone can see how great God is and how much He has done. Paul wants them to remove the shame of what was and celebrate the glory of what is.

Mr. Awesome and I had been married for about two weeks when we realized that we had made a huge mistake. I remember standing on a street corner in Chicago, while we were still on our honeymoon, looking over at Mr. Awesome and realizing the gravity of our situation. We had messed everything up. We were great friends, best friends but this whole marriage thing was a colossal mistake. We spent five long months hiding our marital misery when, thankfully, one of my co-workers recognized that we were in distress. She wasted no time in introducing us to her husband, a pastor in our community, who then spent the next ten months counseling us.

He led us in a pre-marital counseling course and taught us the basics of marital communication. He broke through our misconceptions and schooled us each in our roles and responsibilities in marriage. He taught us how to fight fair, how to disagree but still be in unity and what expectations to place on God and what expectations to place on each other. In short, he stepped neck deep into our mess and helped us find our way out.

It was during those months of counseling that we realized we had a choice to make. We could continue to play the role of Perfect Newlywed Christians or we could get real and be honest about our journey to wedded bliss. We could selfishly gloss over the unlovely bits of our story or we could be real about how much God had done in our life and in our marriage. We could be ashamed of where we were or we could celebrate how far we'd come but we couldn't do both.

The decision wasn't that hard to make, really. We are who we are by the grace of God and hiding where we started would rob Him of the glory of where we are now. We wrote ourselves a note and stuck it to our fridge so we wouldn't forget our commitment to living true. *Our shame is the enemy of someone else's success.*

We dropped the masks we had so painstakingly crafted and we talked about the great work God had done, and was continuing to do, in our hearts and in our relationship. We basked in the glory of all that our loving Father had done and we did our best to reflect that glory to those around us. Not everyone was ready for us unmasked. For some the brightness of God's glory was too harsh in light of their own circumstances and carefully honed images but we didn't let that drive us back behind the veil. We made every effort to live as a testament to the transforming power of His love.

We have tried in every situation and season to live openly and honestly. It has always been our wish that others may be spared heartache and find hope in our journey. If one person can discover God's faithfulness through our story then everything we've gone through, every storm we've survived, and every victory we've claimed has been worth the struggle.

People cannot see how far God has brought us if they don't know where we started. Our testimony has the power to draw people near to God. It can highlight His goodness and faithfulness in specific areas that can speak to the very heart of those listening. Our testimony is the before and after proof of a life transformed by the love of God. That is why we must put words to all that He has done in and through us.

Now for the disclaimer: you can share where you've come from without airing all your dirty laundry. When I was a teen there was a series of Christian books that were very popular. The writer highlighted the lives of prostitutes, drug dealers and run-aways. In the final chapter of each book the main character came to Christ but that was after 20 chapters of drugs, sex, alcohol and just about every other destructive lifestyle choice imaginable. The books were 90% debauchery and 10% Jesus and even as a young teen that felt more than a little off to me. It's important to talk about the miraculous work God has done without glorifying your sin. Make sure your story is more about Him than about you.

When we share our story, when we have the opportunity to reflect the glory of God at work in our lives we need to be sure our story is more about how good God is than how bad we were. People find their way to salvation by understanding God's nature and they will only understand His nature if we acknowledge, celebrate and reflect His glory with unveiled faces and open hearts.

Chapter Twenty-One

THE HOPE CHAIN

2 Corinthians 1:3&4

Blessed be the God and Father of our Lord Jesus Christ, the Father of mercies and God of all comfort who comforts us in all our tribulation that we may be able to comfort those who are in any trouble with the comfort with which we ourselves are comforted by God

I don't know about you but when life gets rough and challenges threaten to overwhelm me, my first instinct is not to thank God. I know all the scriptures about being thankful in every circumstance and the rewards for suffering for His glory but still, when I'm in crisis, "Bless God" is not the first phrase that comes to mind. My instinctual response to disaster usually involves whining and complaining but I'm learning. Life experience and God's grace are working on me and I'd say that thankfulness is now one of my top three reactions to hardship. So, at least that's something.

This hasn't been an easy lesson to learn. It's taken time and maturity to figure out that perspective is everything when you're living through difficult times. I've learned that when we look at hardships from the perspective of what it's doing to us, of course it's going to be a drag. When we feel assaulted, abused and targeted unjustly our righteous indignation gets all fired up and we push back against whomever we feel is to blame for the hell we're going through. But if we stop for a second and look at the bigger picture we just might get a totally different view of the situation. When we understand that what we are experiencing in the moment can impact someone else for eternity it just might make our suffering a little easier to bear.

I was 16 years old when I first caught a glimpse of the big picture. It was Grey Cup Sunday and I was spending the afternoon watching the football game with friends. I had been battling strep throat and a relentless cold for weeks but I was finally on the mend and eager to get out of the house to hang out with my pals.

We were all lounging around a friends' basement, playing crokinole and watching our hometown team get whipped by our western rivals, when I started to feel ill again. I was inexplicably exhausted, my tongue was numb and I suddenly had a splitting headache. My pal, Aaron, who had given me a ride that afternoon, was the first of my friends to notice that I wasn't doing well but it didn't take long for others to jump in and panic.

Aaron rushed me home and within hours my parents had me at the emergency room. The numbness I was experiencing in my tongue had spread leaving all the muscles on the left side of my face paralyzed. My eye was droopy, my mouth sagged and my speech was slurred. Initially the doctors were concerned that I had had a stroke but a neurological assessment determined that I had Bell's Palsy. The tissue around the nerves that control my facial muscles had swollen, probably from my prolonged bout of Strep throat, and that interfered with the nerves' ability to function properly. This condition wasn't fatal but it was potentially permanent.

So, I was 16 years old girl with a partially paralyzed face that led to an alternating leaky/crusty eye, an issue with drooling and slurred speech. Very attractive. This whole messy situation was a total self-esteem killer and I was anything but thankful. I was hurt, angry, humiliated and confused, and I asked myself why was this happening to me? I was a good girl, a Jesus girl, a church girl; I didn't deserve this! All I wanted to do was crawl into a hole and never come out again. I wanted to hide from the outside world but my magnificent friends wouldn't let me.

My friends started to show up at my house unannounced to drag me out to youth group, parties and church. They forced me to socialize. They surrounded me with people who liked me despite my Quasimodo appearance. They prayed for me, lovingly teased me and protected me. They made a paralyzed face seem normal, if not a little bit cool. They loved me past my moodiness, my self-pity and my doubt. They reminded me of who I was and helped me to forget about what I looked like. Their friendship and encouragement made the months it took for my face to heal fly by.

The following summer these same wonderful friends and I went on a two-week mission trip to Mexico to rebuild a church and run a daily children's program. We also hosted nightly church services in the town square. It was at one of these church services one evening that my friends brought an elderly man over to where I was playing with a group of children. As they approached from across the square, I noticed the man was holding his hand over one side of his face, like he was shielding it from view. He seemed very skittish and less than thrilled to be ushered through the crowded town square. The one eye I could see was full of fear, anger and suspicion.

With the help of a translator, I was told that this man had been hiding in his house for weeks because he had fallen ill with Bell's Palsy. He was ashamed of his appearance and afraid to be seen by his friends and neighbors. He had forced his wife and children to move out of the house so they couldn't witness his shame. But when his neighbors heard that Canadian missionaries were in the community they had forced their way into his house to bring him to us. It was Aaron who happened to meet him first. Aaron immediately shared with him my experience with Bell's Palsy and although the man was skeptical, he insisted on meeting 'the girl who was healed.'

I smiled at him and told him it was true; I did have Bell's Palsy but now I was completely recovered. He touched my face, completely in awe of what he saw. His fingers poked and prodded the left side of my face and soon we were both laughing. Then he started crying. I hugged him and prayed for him. I knew the hurt, the fear, the self-consciousness and the hopelessness he felt. I knew because I had been right where he was. And right there, in that moment, standing in a hot and dusty Mexican town square, embracing a stranger, I thanked God for equipping me with all I needed to bring hope to this man. I thanked God for seeing me through the trial of Bell's Palsy.

That was my first encounter with understanding thankfulness in the face of adversity and it's a lesson I've never forgotten. I have walked through a number of hurts and disappointments in my life and each time I've eventually been able to get to the point of thankfulness because each time I have been able to use my story to relate to and lend hope to someone else.

The revelation of thankfulness for me has always come through relationship with others. I've realized that the real tragedy in difficult circumstances is being locked in my own moment of despair, being unable to see past my own disappointment and reach out to others. A circumstance becomes an occasion for thankfulness when we let God in and share His goodness with others. Hope is a chain built through community, compassion and thankfulness.

I have experienced the heartbreak of miscarriages, the fear of near fatal accidents and the disappointment of unexpected medical diagnoses but I have also seen God's peace, joy and faithfulness reign over every circumstance. I have been able to walk alongside others who have had the same experiences and couple my faith with theirs to help carry them through. And for that, I am eternally thankful.

Chapter Twenty-Two

LIVING BOX-FREE

Matthew 13:57-58

So they were offended at Him. But Jesus said to them, "A prophet is not without honor except in his own country and in his own house." Now, He did not do many mighty works there because of their unbelief.

"That's just how they are."

When strung together, those are five of the most limiting words in the English language. It drives me crazy to hear people blow each other off with a statement like that. There are few things more frustrating and defeating than feeling trapped by the limitations others put on you, based on their perception of who you are or should be. It's bad enough when this happens in our schools, workplaces and communities but when it happens in The Church the outcome can be devastating.

I'm not sure what it is about human nature that strives so hard to label and categorize people, but we all do it. Almost from the moment we meet someone new our brains begin to scramble to define them. We gather information from conversations and encounters and we begin to build a profile for them, a neat little box in our mind to stuff them in.

Each time we encounter them again we confirm the confines of their box and if, by chance, they say or do something that is outside their box we decide to either accept this new behavior and expand the box or we reject this new behavior and stuff them back into the original box.

What I have come to realize is that we generally have no problem expanding the box for negative traits but we'd rather hack off the growth of positive traits with a few sharp words and keep the box as is. This box-building makes relationships easy for us. It helps us to know what to expect, to predict reactions and behavior. And it leaves no room for personal growth. Or grace.

We've all made boxes but we've all also been victims of the box. Each one of us has, at one time or another, tried to grow, mature or change something about ourselves. We've pushed against the confines of the box to better ourselves but, inevitably, someone with sharp words has attempted to hack off our new growth and stuff us back into the definition of us that they are comfortable with. Why is that? Why do we do this to each other? I can guess but I don't know the answer for sure. What I do know is that we're not alone in this. Even Jesus was boxed.

Jesus had been travelling and ministering for a while. He had already established a reputation for teaching and healing wherever He went. So when His travels took Him through His hometown, back to the land of His people, His family, you'd think He'd be preaching and healing like never before. You'd think His hometown crowd would come out in droves to support Him. But you'd be wrong. Instead of receiving His teachings and opening their hearts to His healing, folks from Jesus' hometown immediately set to work constructing His box.

"Hey isn't that Joseph's kid?"

"Yeah, I know his brothers."

"I've known him since he was a baby. I know where he comes from."

"Who does he think he is, showing up here, talking like that."

"That's just Mary's son, Jesus."

The hometown crowd, the people who knew Jesus and His family well, the people who should have welcomed Him as their own, became offended and rejected Him. But why? Was Jesus rude? Did He insult them? Was it something He said? Well, yes. And no.

The things He said, and the way He behaved, were proof that the box they had built for Him was too small. They were upset, not by the things He said but that *He* was the one who said it. Nowhere in this passage does it say they thought Jesus was lying or falsely representing the teachings of God. It doesn't record Him treating others poorly or being self-promoting or unkind. In fact, verse 54 states that the wisdom and mighty works astonished them but they were less astonished by Jesus; the small town kid they thought they knew. It wasn't the wisdom He shared or the mighty works He performed that offended the crowds, it was that Jesus, Mary's kid, the carpenter's boy, was the one speaking and performing these things. It wasn't the message, it was the Messenger.

When you read this passage in the Book of Matthew you can see that the verses on either side of this account are full of rich teaching and amazing miracles. Everywhere Jesus went lives were changed. Everywhere. Except at home. The time He spent in His own hometown was marked with unbelief. He didn't perform any great miracles. He didn't change lives - not because He was unwilling - but because they didn't believe.

This incident is one of the few that are recorded in all four Gospels. It makes me think that this encounter had some kind of significance to it. I've heard this story used in many a sermon

over the years and, more often than not, it was part of some kind of warning against expecting respect. Usually it was used as an example of staying humble and not expecting more honor than you deserve. Even Jesus had people who kept Him in His place. But as I've studied this passage and this incident for myself I think there's a different warning here. Don't be the hometown crowd.

Don't be a Box Builder. A Change Limiter. A Miracle Blocker. A Grace Denier. Don't be the one with the sharp words, waiting to hack off new growth. Don't be the one who misses out on being part of the story because you can't see past your own judgments.

When I read this story I wonder what would have happened if the hometown crowd had been on Jesus' side instead of against Him. I wonder what amazing teachings and miracles would have been recorded if they had just set aside their preconceived notions about who He was and received the truth of what He said. I wonder who was meant to be part of The Good News but missed out because they didn't believe. I wonder.

I wonder what I have missed out on while I was busy building boxes. What well-known friend had a wise word of encouragement, what kid-next-door had a specific message from God for me, what familiar family member was living the very truth of God that I needed to see but because of my perception of who they were I missed out. I wonder how often God has tried to use the familiar to reveal the divine and my own judgmental pride has kept me from being part of the good news.

When Jesus said, "A prophet is not without honor except in His own country and His own house," He wasn't throwing a pity party. He was giving voice to the reality that, in this situation, He was victim of the perceptions of others. He said this not to make people feel sorry for Him, not to keep people humble and not as a commentary on society. He said it as a warning through time for those of us in the hometown crowd. *Don't miss out!*

The unbelief of the hometown crowd didn't stop Jesus' ministry. It just stopped their ability to witness it, to be a part of it.

They boxed *themselves* in and missed out on immeasurable bless-ings that could have been theirs. Jesus went on to the next town and the next, feeding thousands, physically and spiritually. Lives were changed, miracles were performed and Jesus' ministry grew. The hometown crowd missed it all.

I never want to limit God and I never want to miss out on a great work He's doing because of my own insecurities and small mindedness. I've discovered the more I know about who I am in Him, the less I feel threatened by others discovering who they are in Him, too. I don't ever want to be accused of boxing someone in when Jesus is trying to set them free. I don't want my familiarity with someone to ever stifle the call of God on their life. I don't ever want to be the cause of someone moving on to the next town because I was unwilling to believe the changing power of God in their life. I want to live box-free and love box-free so that I can experience all that God has to offer!

Section

Four

This One Life

On June 8, 2012 I was curled up in my bed, sicker than I had ever been in my life. A week earlier I had had my second to last chemo treatment but had yet to bounce back. I was dehydrated, nauseated, head achy, feverish and weak. Mr. Awesome was worried enough to call my mom in for back up and she made the nearly two-hour drive from her house to mine in record time. She sat on my bed and force-fed me soup and frozen grapes for hours. And she prayed.

As I dozed on and off that afternoon, I can remember hearing my mom and Mr. Awesome discussing the options. They wanted to take me to the hospital but that's the last place I wanted to be. I didn't want to be sick and somehow I felt that if I gave in and went to the hospital that I would be admitting that I was, indeed, sick. So I held my ground, stayed in my own bed and said a few prayers of my own.

During the darkest parts of my cancer journey there was one phrase that repeated constantly in the back of my mind, that echoed with every beat of my heart, that I held on to with both hands as I fought this uphill battle: This One Life. It had become abundantly clear to me, as I faced my own mortality, that this was the only chance I had. I only had this one life. That's it. There's no do-overs, no second chances, no reset button. I only have a limited number of minutes on this planet to live, love and make a difference. This One Life.

That was the prayer of my heart on June 8, 2012. *Dear God, let me live this one life. I'm not done yet!* He heard and He answered. I recovered within days and with the help of my awesome Poison

Squad (aka Cancer Team) I did not get that sick again. I finished my radiation treatments and I lived. I am living. This One Life.

As a Jesus follower, I know that I will live for eternity with Him but I also know I have a limited amount of time to collect as many people for Him as I can. I have a flash of time to be an effective ambassador of His love, of the possibilities a life in Him brings. Every day I am faced with the question, "How are you going to live this one life today?" Some days I answer well, I live well and I know that I have made a difference. Other days, not so much. But each day is another chance to answer the question.

Let me ask you, what are you doing with This One Life? How are you living as a Jesus ambassador? Are you living as a Jesus ambassador? The decision to live this life for Jesus is the decision to live intentionally. It's the decision to live obediently, in community and with care. It's the decision to think outside yourself and live so that others may know God.

I have a friend who is a youth pastor and he teaches his youth that there are only two purposes in life; to know God and to make Him known. That's how I plan to live This One Life of mine. I want to know God, to know Him so well that His nature radiates from me and draws others to Him. To know Him and to make Him known. That is how I plan to live This One Life.

Chapter *Twenty-Three*

WHERE YOU ABIDE

John 15:9

As the Father loved Me, I also loved you; abide in My love.

During the early years of our marriage Mr. Awesome and I moved around a lot. We lived in several different places in a couple of different cities. Moving that much seemed like an adventure and I took it all in stride because I knew this gypsy life wouldn't last forever. I knew that eventually the secret dream of my heart would become our reality.

Through all the making do, packing and unpacking and living out of boxes I had a hope for what our life would one day be. I had a dream of having a family, of owning a house, of creating a home. I would fantasize about our little house with a front porch and a cozy feel. I would imagine myself preparing meals, entertaining friends and relaxing in my own home. Just weeks after

Crafty was born, my dream came true when we moved into our first home.

It was everything I had dreamed of. It was small enough to have the right cozy feel but not too small to be functional. Dude had his own room, complete with a window seat overlooking our tree lined front street and Crafty's nursery was as sweet and dreamy as a baby girl's room should be. It was perfect and I couldn't have been more content.

We lived in that little bubble of homey bliss for a couple of years but when we discovered Mischief was on his way, we realized that our lovely, cottagey home just wasn't going to be able to contain us anymore. We were bursting at the seams! Books, toys and other random kid paraphernalia were filling every square inch of our home. It seemed that the bigger the kids got the bigger their mess became and I couldn't see how we would possibly be able to fit another person in that house.

We were very sad the day we turned the keys to this little dream house over to its new owner, especially because we had not yet found a new home for ourselves. We moved back into my parents' house while we continued to house hunt. We had looked at dozens of houses but none of them felt like home and the clock was ticking. I was eight months pregnant, living out of suitcases in my old bedroom at my parents' house with two toddlers and a grouchy husband; I was exhausted and frustrated. In a desperate act of utter exasperation we bought the first house we could both tolerate.

It was a one-hundred-year-old character house with six-inch baseboards, hardwood floors and a decorative arch in the dining room. I was instantly enchanted by the history and potential beauty of the place, despite the hideous wallpaper and nasty carpet in every room. Mr. Awesome was less impressed and more than a little wary of all the work it would take to uncover this 'potential beauty' but he tried to be positive and approached this new adventure with a 'how bad could it be' attitude.

The next six years were the most stressful of our married life. Just about everything that could go wrong with a house did. Water issues were covered up by the previous owners, so we were taken by surprise when a water feature sprouted from the kitchen light fixture. We had sewer back-up that caused thousands of dollars of damage and more than a few moments of intense fellowship between me and Mr. Awesome. While we were in the middle of cleaning up the six inches of sewer water from our basement we discovered our roof was leaking in several places. Upon further investigation we realized it wasn't a regular leak, it was ice damming and the plaster walls in that area of the house were saturated beyond repair. That resulted in us having to gut the whole back of our house and renovate our kitchen and laundry room in addition to repairing our roof.

While gutting the kitchen we discovered there was no insulation on the main floor, save the three-foot by four-foot wasps' nest that the contractors discovered in the wall. They laughingly dubbed it 'wasp-alation.' But we weren't laughing because all of this was on top of the 'regular' house issues we were constantly dealing with. Issues such as, our yard turning into a swamp each spring, the finicky plumbing, the sketchy electrical, the temperamental furnace and the drafty windows.

Six years into this misadventure we had done extensive renovations but the house still needed much more work before it could be considered complete. We were stressed, financially strapped, desperately unhappy and in a constant state of chaos. We hated our house and we hated our life. We would get up early on a Saturday and rush out to nowhere in particular, just so we wouldn't have to be at home. We would drive around aimlessly, for hours, just so we wouldn't have to stay in our house. When we were at home, more often than not, we would either bicker about everything that needed to be done and all the things that were wrong in our life. There was no peace and little rest for us in that house.

Somewhere along the way, we had an epiphany. We realized that we didn't have to live in that house. No one was forcing us to live in a leaky, drafty, broken-down house. We could live in a different house. We could move – and we did!

We bought a house with a solid foundation, a watertight roof and a beautiful yard. Our home went from being a loathsome place of stress and strife to a welcoming place of refuge. Suddenly we liked our house; we liked being at home. For the first time in years home meant something good; it meant safety, security and peace. When we chose a different place to live our definition of home changed.

As we settled into our new home, we realized that more than just our address and sense of well-being could change. We could change us, our life, our purpose. We were free to choose a new definition for our life in general; the things we didn't like about ourselves, our character, our perspective could change, too. We realized, too, that if we didn't make this change, all the negativity of the old house would move with us into the new house because the house wasn't the core of the problem, our attitude was. We had replaced peace with stress and love with hate so the only way back to a life we loved was to reverse the tide.

Over time and through God's Word we were reminded that Jesus invites us to live in the safety and security of His love. *Abide in My love.* Abide means to take up residence, to live. Jesus wants us to enter into His love, settle down and make ourselves at home, to live there, in His love. And He extends the same invitation to you.

He wants you to feel the all-encompassing power of His love, also. He wants you to claim its protection, its gentleness and its security for your own. He wants you to experience the permanent, steadfastness of His love. He wants you to rest in it. He wants His love to be your home.

Abiding in Jesus' love is a decision you make daily, sometimes minute-by-minute. It's deciding that no matter the circumstance you will hold tight to the truth that Jesus' love surrounds you, covers you and fills you. And just as moving into a more secure house didn't ensure us a problem-free life, choosing to abide in the love of Jesus won't make you immune to life and all of its hazards. Tough times will come and storms will still rage but when you abide in Jesus, in His love, you will have a place of safety to retreat to, a secure place to wait out the storm. You will have the confidence of knowing that you are never alone, of knowing that you are with Him and He is with you. That you are abiding.

Chapter *Twenty-Four*

A CHANGE OF HEART

Psalm 51:16 & 17

For You do not desire sacrifice or else I would give it; You do not delight in burnt offering. The sacrifices of God are a broken spirit and a contrite heart – these, O God, You will not despise.

I'm a pretty serious *Anne of Green Gables* fan. The first time I read *Anne* was when I was about ten years old. My grandmother gave me her copy of the story, the one she bought on the ship from England to Canada when she was a young war bride. I remember opening the pages of that old book and being immediately drawn into the story of the feisty red-headed orphan who found her place in the world by accident. I devoured that book in record time and when I was finished, I went right back to the beginning and read it all over again.

I love Anne's quirkiness and her flare for the dramatic. Those two traits collide in a fabulous catastrophe that is one of my very favorite Anne moments ever. Anne had lost her temper and insulted her new neighbor, Rachel Lynde. Even though Anne felt completely justified in her anger and not the least bit sorry for her outburst, she agreed to apologize to Mrs. Lynde so that Marilla, Anne's new mother, could save face. But it was no ordinary apology that Anne gave.

The whole way to The Lynde's house Anne planned out and rehearsed what she was going to say. The moment she arrived on the Lynde's porch, Anne dropped to her knees in a very dramatic fashion. Using the most flowery words possible, Anne delivered the most self-berating, penitent apology one had ever heard. The thing is, Anne didn't mean a word of what she said, she just wanted to appear sorry so the people she cared about wouldn't be angry with her anymore. She put on a show of repentance without having repentance ever touch her heart and although Mrs. Lynde bought the performance, Marilla knew Anne was faking.

I think the reason why I love this Anne moment so much is that I can identify with her. I hate it when people are mad at me and I'd do just about anything to smooth things over. This is doubly true when it comes to my relationship with God and I don't think I'm alone in this. Many of us live from Anne moment to Anne moment with Him. When we trip up, disobey or behave contrary to how we know God desires us to behave we make a show of apologizing. We scramble to set things right even if we're not entirely ready to apologize. We come to the altar humbled and teary-eyed believing that the outward display of sorrow for our wrong-doing will be enough. We show God our sacrifice of obedience. We *show* but that's as far as the repentance goes and God knows it.

Our sacrifice is hollow. It's meaningless because we haven't allowed the repentance to go heart deep. Outwardly we go through the motions of appearing contrite but internally we feel completely justified in our sin. We hold on to our right to be right, like a spoiled child, and act out our apology as if we're fooling God. We are the fools, though. God knows fully the difference between a genuine and contrite heart and the charade of sacrifice and He isn't willing to just play along. A façade isn't enough for Him, He wants the real thing from us.

When I introduced Crafty to *Anne of Green Gables* we started with the made-for-television mini-series. Crafty was just as captivated with this Anne girl as I was at her age. It was a joy to watch her watch Anne with such rapt attention. She laughed at all the same parts that made me chuckle and she empathized with Anne just as I did, and still do, but Crafty caught me a little off guard when she noticed something I had never given much thought to.

"Why are the buildings like that?" she asked.

"Like what?"

"Like that, with really tall fronts but nothing behind it. Its all empty back there."

"That's how they made buildings back then. They built up the front to make the building seem bigger, more impressive than it really was," I answered.

"Why didn't they just build the whole thing big?" she asked.

"Too expensive. This way they could make their town look fancier while keeping the cost down. Lots of towns were built that way," I answered, hoping she'd drop this bizarre line of questioning so we could go back to enjoying the show.

"Yeah, but if everyone knows it's fake then who are they trying to impress?" she persisted.

"I'm not sure. I think they all just agree to pretend to not notice the buildings are fake."

"They all agreed to believe a lie? Weird."

It is weird and so are we. How often are our sacrifices just like those old buildings? How often do we build a façade and think that the appearance of repentance is enough for God? How often do we weigh the cost of a genuine change of heart against the benefits we'll receive or the work we'd have to do? How often do we settle for going through the motions and accept the same from those around us? How often do we agree to believe the lie from ourselves and from others?

Real change is very costly. To change, to become more Christ-like, will always cost us something. As we move closer to Him we have to move further away from the things that keep us from Him. Our genuine repentance and change of heart may require us to step away from friends, habits or routines that have become part of who we are; we have to be willing to stop pretending. And that, at times, can be costly and painful for us.

Psalm 51:16 & 17 lays out God's expectations pretty clearly, though. He doesn't want a show, He's not looking to be entertained and He can't be fooled. God doesn't want to pretend that we are His. He wants the real deal. He wants to see our hearts really and truly break for the things that break His, He wants His heartbeat to be ours. He wants us to be His. Pure. Simple. Real.

We can take this heart issue a step further, past personal repentance, to how we live our everyday life in community. Do our hearts truly respond to the needs we see in our community or do we just put on the appearance of caring? Do our hearts respond to the things of God or do we merely respond to social trends? Do we allow the injustice in the world to spur us into action or do we keep these causes as fashion statements?

Social justice has become cool. It's trendy to wear a cause-sponsored shirt or fashionable shoes from a company that helps kids in need. It's hip to do a water walk or collect change for change but do we allow the truth behind the cause to pierce our hearts and change us? Do we allow the plight of the people God so loves to affect us at a heart level? It's not enough to appear changed when the possibility of actually being changed is right within our grasp ... we just have to be willing to let go of what was and step into the genuine moment of what is.

The bottom line is, God doesn't want a display of all the right moves. He's not impressed by a well-choreographed dance of repentance or a fashionable spectacle of caring. He is not willing to pretend with us. He wants a genuine reaction from a broken and contrite heart. That is a sacrifice He will cherish. That is the heart He can change.

Chapter *Twenty-Five*

LIVING THE EXAMPLE

Deuteronomy 6:5-7

> *You shall love the Lord your God with all your heart, with all your soul, and with all your strength. And these words which I command you today shall be in your heart. You shall teach them diligently to your children and shall talk of them when you sit in your house, when you walk by the way, when you lie down and when you rise up.*

Train up a child in the way he should go and when he is old he will not depart from it (Proverbs 22:6). But Jesus said, "Let the little children come to Me, and do not forbid them; for such is the kingdom of Heaven." (Matthew 19:14). He who spares the rod hates his son, but he who loves him disciplines him promptly (Proverbs 13:24). And Jesus increased in wisdom and stature, and in favor with God and men (Luke 2:52). When it comes to discussing child raising, these are some of the most common scriptures quoted. And some of the least helpful.

In our church culture we are quick to tell parents what they should do but no one seems to have a clear idea of how to do it. I remember being a new parent, and as with most other people in my position, I was just thankful to make it through the day with the same number of kids I started with and with no major injuries or damages to report. Anything my kids happened to learn along the way was purely coincidental, a happy accident. Not exactly intentional parenting but it was the best we could do at the time.

During this time of our parenting life we would often hear pastors use those familiar child-rearing scriptures to urge parents to do better or more to equip their children for the future. I would furiously scribble notes, nodding and amening along the way. But at the end of the sermon I was no closer to understanding how to equip my kids than I was at the beginning of the message. I grew frustrated and a wee bit frantic. I felt as though I were letting my kids down with each day that passed by not teaching them some kind of fundamental, yet profound, Biblical truth. This led to many failed attempts at modeling the Perfect Christian Home.

When our kids were very young we tried to them read stories from their picture Bible and sing Sunday School songs before bed. But this was a flop. I couldn't handle the singsong language and dumbed-down versions of my favorite Bible stories. I quickly became bored with my part in this bedtime routine. For his part, Mr. Awesome gave the Sunday school songs a try, but having not attended Sunday school himself, he knew very few church songs and usually ended up singing the kids a Christmas Carol/Classic Rock hybrid.

I built a 'Fruit of the Spirit' tree and a flannel-graph station in our playroom, complete with little Bible dudes and repositionable fruit. On rainy days I'd coax the kids into acting out their favorite Bible stories or I would quiz them on their Sunday School lessons. Despite my best efforts my preschoolers were not grasping the importance of a solid Biblical foundation so I gave up – for a time.

We gave intentional churching another try when our kids were all in school. We set aside time to read from a family devotional and pray together but our conversations never seemed to go as planned. Inevitably, someone would look at someone else and that would start an argument, or someone would pass gas and everyone would get the giggles; someone would have an elaborate 'what if' story (for example, what if a dinosaur crashed through our living room window or what if I wasn't born me and I was born someone else?) and derail the conversation. Whenever we'd try to get back to the scripted questions from the book the conversation became forced and contrived because it was.

It was in the midst of this latest failed Home Bible Learning that I ran into an old friend. As we chatted about our growing up years I remembered how her family always did a devotional together every morning and had a family prayer time before bed every night. When I asked her how her parents were able to maintain this tradition and teach her and her siblings to make God a priority in their lives she laughed – and not a joyful laugh.

She said that her parents made these traditions important but they didn't make God important. She said that she always felt like she had to perform growing up; she had to be the perfect Christian girl and do and say all of the right things. She felt pressure to uphold the carefully crafted image her parents had created. They read a devo every morning and recited a prayer together every night but, from her perspective, God didn't factor into any of the in between moments. She felt as though she was taught how to play a role but not live a life devoted to God.

She ended our conversation telling me of the years she spent drinking, partying and sleeping around and that she still struggled with the idea of God being a real Being who loved her. "Whatever you do, Nic, be real about it. If you really love God, let your kids see that."

Truthfully, that exchange freaked me out. I certainly didn't want to present an image that would eventually cause my kids to

turn away from the very God I wanted them to have a relationship with. I was so afraid of scarring the kids with religious tradition that I stopped forcing the routine of family devotions and
contrived prayer times. I was so unsure of what to do that I did
nothing. We prayed for the kids at bedtime and that was it.

I wrestled with the guilt of being an inadequate Christian
parent for quite a while. Whenever I was at play dates and moms
would start comparing how much their kids knew about Jesus,
how the kids independently prayed for one another all the time
and how these precious spiritual prodigies held a spontaneous
neighborhood tent revival in the sandbox at the park, I would
smile and nod and pray a frantic prayer that my kids would not
choose this moment to try out a Harry Potter spell on one of their
little friends or sing one of the slightly inappropriate Rod Stewart
songs their grandfather had taught them. I resigned myself to the
fact that I was less than a Perfect Christian Mom and hoped that
enough holiness from these tots would rub off on my wee hea-
thens to save them.

Once I relaxed and stopped trying to be Robo-Christian Mom a
wonderful thing started happening in our family. My kids started
asking questions about God and the Bible. They started cuddling
up with me as I watched church podcasts or read from my Bible.
I would frequently catch Dude reading his Bible to Mischief or
walk in on Crafty singing along to worship music in her room.
Our dinner table conversations often became about God, what we
were each learning about Him and how He is so good and faithful. God became part of our everyday, living, eating, breathing,
playing, loving lives.

When I read this passage from Deuteronomy everything suddenly made sense. Moses didn't tell the Israelites to take their kids
to the temple once a week so the priest could tell them about God.
He didn't tell them to throw pop quizzes at them and force them
to re-enact God's greatest hits. Moses reminded the Israelites to

love God and to let their kids see them love God with their whole hearts everyday. And it's the same for us.

We can't just take our kids to God's house. We have to bring God into our homes. We have to make God an everyday, extraordinary God. We have to make the God of the universe into the Father of our hearts. That's how we train up our children, how we guide them and how we help them grow in wisdom, stature and in favor with God and men.

Chapter *Twenty-Six*

BEING NOT DOING

Hebrews 10:24 & 25

And let us consider one another in order to stir up love and good works, not forsaking the assembling of ourselves together, as is the manner of some, but exhorting one another, and so much the more as you see the Day approaching.

When I was a kid, there was this show on television I just loved. It was a sci-fi show, called *Quantum Leap*. It was about this physicist who gets stuck in an endless loop of time travel where he is injected into the life and body of a person and is made to right a wrong. Each week the main character landed in a different point in history, in a different body and at a different age. My favorite thing about the show was how he had to just blend in wherever he was and make things work. I admired his adaptability, his capacity to be everything to everyone, to blend into the crowd. That was the way to do life, or so I thought.

Over time this became my M.O. for Christianity. Somewhere in my teen years my desire to fit in clashed with my church upbringing, which, at times, strayed from the Jesus Freak model and wandered into the Just Plain Freak mode. I was bothered by some of the weird things I saw in church and I didn't know how to separate my faith in God from the strangeness in the church so I began to lead a dual life.

With my Christian friends I was all in. I was the image of a connected, maturing Christian teen. I really did love Jesus with my whole heart but I wanted to keep all that love on the inside. I didn't want to risk any weirdness slipping out when I was with my unchurched friends so I did my best to separate my two lives. I was still a moral, 'good' girl but sans the Jesus part. I was just like the *Quantum Leap* guy. I did regular life then I did church life and preferably the two paths stayed separate. I was the person I needed to be in whatever situation I was in. I was a wholehearted, undercover, Jesus follower.

I lived this Jesus Spy life for a lot of years. I was completely sold out for Jesus but I didn't want to be weird so I tried to keep my Christian life under wraps outside of the church walls. I didn't know how to be a Jesus girl in a secular world so I went underground. I hid and only spoke of my faith when I was absolutely sure that everyone within earshot was on the same page as me. I didn't want to be offensive or preachy. I just wanted to do my life and that, essentially, was the problem.

I stopped living my life. Instead I compartmentalized my life and 'did' it in different spheres. I did family, did friends, did community, and did church. I did all the things in my life but none of them were connected with each other. It became easy to *Quantum Leap* my life without really engaging with anyone, without really connecting, without really making my relationship with Jesus a part of my everyday life. I could get away with doing church, doing life, doing lunch, doing, doing, doing and never being. Never really living.

As long as I kept my Jesus relationship casual I could maintain this covert ops style of Christianity. Jesus was for Sundays, for crisis and for meal times. The rest of the time it was okay to be a 'normal' person. The rest of the time I could be just like everyone else and do my life my way. Somewhere along the way, though, this became not enough for me. I felt as though I was living a half-life, like I was missing out on something really, really good.

A few years ago something started rumbling in my spirit. I had started to read my Bible, listen to teaching podcasts and worship music. I began to pray outside of meal times and when there was nothing going wrong. I began to have a real relationship with Jesus and it changed me. I began to see that being a Christian everyday didn't necessarily mean being weird, that it was possible to live my faith in a way that drew me closer to other people instead of setting me at a distance from them.

As my relationship with Jesus grew certain words and phrases began to really irritate me. I'm a word person and I fully believe that words have power to shape circumstances and frame your life. I believe that the meaning of words, individually or strung together in a sentence, carries a hefty weight. Words should never be tossed around carelessly. So it was from this perspective that this popular Christian idea of 'doing' became one of the trigger points of my inner volcano.

The phrases 'doing church' and 'doing life' became very popular in contemporary Christian culture a number of years ago but they've never sat right with me. 'Doing' is a task word. It's a busy word that describes accomplishing a certain task and that's not how I see church or life. When we categorize these important aspects of our life as items on our 'to do' list, as if they held no more importance than grocery shopping or doctor's appointments, we give ourselves permission to compartmentalize our lives and our interactions with others. This compartmentalization of our lives excuses us from encountering one another and allowing the life force of Jesus to penetrate our souls and reach into every area of our lives.

'Doing' instead of 'being' and 'living' robs us of experiencing the life that God has imagined for us, a life of His divine love and community. Here's the thing, we don't do church; we are The Church. We don't do life; we live life. We don't do relationship, we have relationship, we are in relationship. Our faith in Jesus is a living, breathing life force that we are meant to share, not some feel-good Christianese movement that we 'do' once a week for an hour. We live the Jesus life as The Church, in community. We let His life overflow into every area of our life and we become His ambassadors wherever we go. That's how we are meant to live this one life we have.

When this understanding hit me it changed everything. When my spirit awoke to the truth that Jesus didn't just save me from hell but He set me free so that I may show others the way to freedom in Him, everything about how I lived my life changed. I stopped doing church and started being The Church. I let Jesus out of the pew and took Him with me into the schools, grocery stores, community meetings and coffee dates I went to. I let Jesus be everything to everyone and I just became me, a wife, mother, friend and Jesus follower.

Quantum Leap is a cool idea for a sci-fi show but it's no way to live our lives. There is no possible way to be everything to everyone and Jesus doesn't want us to just blend in. God has called us to be in the world, not of the world (John 17:14 & 15). That means He wants us wholly engaged in the life that surrounds us while being wholly in Him. He wants us to be ambassadors of His love. Ambassadors don't give up their citizenship just because they are in another country and they don't get weird. They live each and everyday as examples, as messengers, of the one whose banner they carry. We are God's ambassadors; we carry His name, His banner of love. We get to live this life loving The Church and being The Church. No more doing, just being.

Chapter *Twenty-Seven*

IT's WHAT WE'RE KNOWN FOR

Philippians 4:5

Let your gentleness be known to all men. The Lord is at hand.

The apostle Paul is writing to the Philippian church at a very exciting time in history. Christianity is growing. People are converting from Judaism and paganism in droves. Christ followers are hunted and persecuted for their beliefs and Paul, the lead pastor of all these zealous new believers, is attempting to shape the identity of Christians in the world. He wants to encourage their passion but he also recognizes a need for something more than zeal, something that will set The Church apart from the current culture.

The culture of the time was not so unlike ours. People had developed an insatiable bloodlust. Their entertainment revolved around violent sport and the religious leaders of the day were just as power hungry as the politicians. The population worshipped themselves, what they could acquire and their social standing above all else.

They loved to work themselves into a frenzy, they loved the thrill of emotion but paid little attention to the cause behind the emotion. They were aggressive, self-seeking and godless.

Paul understood the culture because it wasn't long before the writing of this letter that he had been right in the middle of it. Paul had once been Saul, a pious, aggressive, emotionally driven religious leader that so many people in that culture aspired to be. He had been one of them and that helped him to fully appreciate the transformation power of a life in Christ offered.

It is from this perspective that he writes to The Church in Philippi. He fills the first half of the letter reminding this church to be the difference in the world, to be the light of Jesus wherever they are and to keep pressing forward for the call of Christ. He encourages them through their suffering for the cause of Christ and commends them for all that they have accomplished in His name. It's all very uplifting and motivational. It's the kind of narrative that stirs the heart, builds faith and inspires people to action. And just as these words are pushing your drive to do something, to be something in this world, Paul tells The Church to be gentle.

What?

The first time I read this verse I remember thinking how odd it was that this is the thing Paul wants The Church to be known for but as I reread the chapter I began to understand what Paul was getting at. He wanted The Church to pursue the call of Christ but not in the way the world operated. He didn't want violence, aggression and force to be the way of The Church just as it was the way of the world. He wanted something different, something more for Christ followers. He wanted them to be Christ-like.

I grew up in a denomination that was all fire and passion and movement. We picketed abortion clinics, preached on street corners and spent a lot of time working ourselves into a holy frenzy. We were constantly 'on the move' 'chasing God's best' with a 'holy passion.' It was all very exciting but in the midst of all this chasing and fire and holiness we became like freight trains, barreling full speed ahead. We were loud, obnoxious and, at times, weird. Our love and passion were genuine but our method of delivery was off the mark.

Over time we mellowed, outwardly, but in private, among ourselves we still had this culture of movement, of looking for the next big thing. There was still a sense of panic that God might move without you so you better hurry up. There was a constant worry that if you didn't move, you were going to miss God and then where would you be? As time passed, I entered my thirties, still not used significantly by God – or so I thought – so, I resigned myself to the reality that I had somehow missed God. I wasn't vigilant enough, I wasn't watching, I wasn't moving and so He went on without me. I was disappointed in myself and felt relegated to life on the Christian backbench.

A few years ago, my perspective on all this completely changed. God dropped me smack dab in the middle of a Gentle People and I was astonished. These people waited. On God. They relaxed into Him and His plan. There was no hurry, no panic, no frantic movement. There was no mad rush; God wasn't going anywhere without them. God had a plan for us and if we remained obedient it was all good. Time was never going to run out because God is eternal.

Now, like Pastor Cam used to say, for every mile of road there's two miles of ditch. There is such a thing as being so at rest in God that you actually fall asleep and that's not what we want either. We do need to be alert and ready when God calls us into action. But we don't need to panic. There is something to be said for peace, for being secure in the truth of who Jesus is and who you are in Him. There is something to be said for living in gentle trust.

I am all for allowing the presence of God to fill us, to change us, to inspire us with a holy purpose but we must never forget why we were saved in the first place. It was for freedom that Christ set us free. It is for the purpose of bringing the lost into His embrace that we ourselves were found. I may not know much about evangelizing but I do know a few things about relationship;

the first being hate, fear and force never draw people into relationship. Love, peace and gentleness do. Ah, gentleness. There's that word again.

Paul knew exactly what he was doing when he included the call to gentleness in this letter. Anyone can get fired up with righteous fervor. Anyone can pound a pulpit and make radical statements. Anyone can storm the gates and tear down strongholds but God's people are called to more than that. They are called to love, nurture and rebuild. They are called to be the very heart of Jesus to the lost and hurting.

I can be a fairly intense person. I get my game face on and then all bets are off. I get focused on something I'm passionate about and I will talk over, around and through anyone I need to in order to have my voice heard and get my point across. I can steam roll the opposition and turn anyone with a differing opinion into road kill and more often than not I can push until I get my way. But how Christ-like is that?

It's not. I have had to learn to channel my passion and my sense of justice appropriately. I have had to remind myself for whom I am fighting and who is the real enemy. I have had to temper my sense of purpose with God's call to unity. In short, I have had to be schooled in gentleness. And in learning to be gentle I have seen the endless blessings that gentleness brings.

Gentleness has brought me friendships, opened my heart and expanded my capacity to love. Gentleness has introduced me to other perspectives; it has allowed me to see value in things I might have previously dismissed as insignificant. Gentleness has brought me community in a way that passion and conviction alone never could have done. Gentleness has made me approachable, it has softened me, removed some of my rough edges.

I love that Paul, perhaps the most radical, passionate and hardcore believer in the history of The Church, saw the value of being gentle. The fact that this gnarly, fiery guy came to understand and live gentleness gives me hope that I, too, can be known for my gentleness, that I, too, can be more Christ-like.

Chapter *Twenty-Eight*

REACHING PAST THE MOMENT

Philippians 3:12-14

Not that I have already attained or am already perfected; but I press on, that I may lay hold of that which Christ Jesus has also laid hold of me. Brethren, I do not count myself to have apprehended; but one thing I do, forgetting those things which are behind and reaching forward to those things which are ahead, I press toward the goal for the prize of the upward call of God in Christ Jesus.

When I read the book of Philippians, I can almost hear the apostle Paul shouting through time and right into our current age. He wastes no words on niceties and flattery. He doesn't soften up the crowd with a little joke or cute anecdote. He just jumps right in with the message that is bursting from his heart for The Church and it's a message that is still so relevant today; "Just let go and move on!"

This a love letter … with a kick. God wants His people to know that He isn't finished with them, that salvation wasn't the finish line. It's actually just the beginning. God, through Paul, encourages The Church that He has this great big life for them to live together. He wants them to know that He has designed them to be a community of Light Bearers in the dark world that surrounds them, that He desires unity and peace for them, that there is a prize to be attained but it is not for this life or of this world. He wants them to let go of what they know and reach for Him and He reminds them that their reach only extends so far while they are holding tight to what is in the past. And the same is true for us.

There is nothing sadder than someone who is locked in a moment of their own history. People who have experienced a significant moment in life can end up setting up camp there. They can allow that one moment in time to shape their life story and define them. To limit them. A moment that was only ever meant to be part of their story becomes their whole story. It becomes their point of reference and every other experience in their life is measured against that one significant moment.

This life-defining moment doesn't necessarily have to be a bad moment either. People get trapped in former glories as easily as past failures. Look at the over-zealous hockey dad who was a star just shy of NHL fame in his day, or the overbearing stage mom who held the lead role in every play her high school produced during her time. People like this have held tight to the moment of their biggest triumph, greatest popularity or closest brush with fame at the cost of their future success.

You might be thinking, "Good thing I've never been successful. I have nothing to hold on to!" Don't kid yourself. The snare of missed opportunities holds just as tight as the one of former glories. I have met just as many people who have allowed themselves to be trapped in what-could-have-been thinking as those who are reliving High School victories. We can allow what didn't happen to define us just as easily as what did happen. The good news is that we don't have to fall into either trap. We have a third option. We can just let go and press forward.

I love how Paul words this. Basically he tells The Church that he's not perfect and that he doesn't have all the answers but there is one thing he has sorted out, one thing he understands and practices daily. He has discovered the value and freedom in letting go. He has realized the importance of releasing whatever is in the past and moving forward into the life God has prepared for him. He acknowledges that there is something in the future, just outside of his grasp waiting for him. This 'something' is the life that Jesus has already claimed for him and is holding out to him. Jesus has brought it within his reach but Paul still has to do some legwork to grab hold of it for himself.

It's kind of like being in a scavenger hunt. You receive the first clue at the starting line. It invites you to participate with the promise of a wonderful prize at the end. But you have to choose whether you want to give this scavenger hunt a go or not. You can sit down, ponder the meaning of the clue and the validity of the promise of the prize or you can move forward. You take the risk and choose to move forward, to take the first step toward the goal of the prize.

You let the clue lead you to the designated spot and there you find the second clue. You can choose now to keep moving forward to the next clue and the next or you can sit down on the path and refuse to move. You can let the disappointment of not attaining the prize overwhelm you and keep you stuck at this clue box. You can sit there, telling all who pass by, what a sham this race is.

Or maybe you're not disappointed. Maybe you are super excited that you solved the first clue. Maybe this is the moment of your greatest triumph so you set up a roadside attraction to declare to all who pass by that you have had great success in solving the first clue. The truth is, you are just as stuck as your neighbor who is wallowing in disappointment. Neither of you will actually attain the real prize because it can only be found in letting go, pressing on and moving forward.

Reading this you may be thinking *Sure, easy for you to say. You haven't lived my life.* And it's true, I haven't lived your life but I've lived mine. I have walked through heartaches and disappointments that have nearly overwhelmed me. Circumstances have occurred that could have easily dragged me into an irrevocable depression. I have also had moments of intense joy and triumph, moments that I could spend my life replaying in my mind while the whole world passed me by. Each person lives their life with highs and lows and it's up to each one of us to accept the truth of Paul's words and put them to the test in our own lives.

In the beginning, letting go isn't easy. It's scary and overwhelming to think of living life without the security of That One Moment wrapped around us. We fear that if we let go it might mean we didn't care or love or feel enough in our moment of sorrow or that we might never again know the joy of sweet success like we did in That One Moment. In the beginning it is difficult but the thing is, each time you let go it gets easier to do it again.

Back to the scavenger hunt analogy: As you move from marker to marker you realize that you are getting faster, stronger and more agile. You gain energy, enthusiasm and excitement as you realize you get closer to the prize with each marker you pass. You still carry the joy and sorrows of past experiences with you but they don't weigh you down or hold you back anymore because you have set your eye on the prize and you won't be denied!

I'm not perfect and I don't have it all figured out but this is one thing I do know, moving forward toward all that Jesus has for me is way better than being stuck in a moment of my own history. I can't do it in my own strength, but I don't have to. Jesus wants to run this race, do this scavenger hunt, with me. And He wants to be there for you, too … and that's Good News!

Chapter Twenty-Nine

SEEING THE INTANGIBLE

Joshua 18:3

Then Joshua said to the children of Israel, "How long will you neglect to go and possess the land which the Lord God of your fathers has given you?"

The children of Israel had spent 45 years walking, wandering and warring. God had spent a generation proving Himself and raising up His children to trust in Him. Five of those 45 years had been spent in the land that had been promised. For five years, the Israelites had worked to clear and divide the land that God had promised to their fathers. The work was done and yet there they were, still sitting and waiting. Not one of them had begun to really live in this land even though they had been raised on the hope of this Promised Land. They, who for generations, had sung about their Deliverer, and now were delivered, seemed more lost than ever.

Joshua had led the children of Israel across the Jordan River and into the land that God had promised to give them. He led the armies in pushing back and destroying the enemies of God's chosen people. He claimed and conquered and then set about dividing the land between the tribes, just as God instructed. Joshua had done his part. He did everything asked of him to bring this promise to reality so why was no one moving in? Why were the children of Israel still camping out instead of moving in? Why didn't they possess what they already rightfully owned?

They didn't know how to possess. I think they knew that they could possess this land, that they should possess it. I even think they wanted to possess it but I don't think they had a hot clue of what 'possessing' looked like or where to start. They needed Joshua to walk them through the steps of making themselves at home in the place they had hoped for, dreamed of and fought for. They needed this one last thing from their leader.

Growing up in an evangelical church I have heard my fair share of sermons on possessing the promises. I know all the catch phrases and scriptures about naming the things that God says He has provided for us and claiming these precious promises. I'm sure you have, too. I think it's pretty safe to assume that, if you've been a believer for longer than five minutes, you know that there is more to this life than what we can achieve on our own - that Jesus has purchased a promised life for us with His life - but how do we *get* this promised life?

Looking at my own life, I recognize things that have kept me from living to the full extent of what God intends. I can see there are certain things, hang-ups and a lack of understanding, that have kept me from walking into my own Promised Land. As I've spent time thinking about this, three distinct hang-ups have come to mind; fear, laziness and confusion.

Fear is the biggest roadblock to anything we want to achieve in life. Fear of the unknown. Fear of change. Fear of failure. Fear of success. We are afraid of what people will say about us. We are afraid of what we will have to leave behind. We are afraid of what we are walking into. We are paralyzed with fear. We are stunted by fear. We lose out because of fear.

I've heard often that faith is the opposite of fear - that if you have enough faith - you'll be able to drive back your fears. That's not true and it's not Biblical. You can believe your worst fear will come true. That's having faith in your fear. No, faith isn't the antidote to fear, love is. 1John 4:18 tells us that perfect love casts out fear. It is trusting in the perfect love of our Father that our fears begin to dissipate. It is abiding in His love that leaves no room for fear.

With fear out of the way, the next thing I trip over is my own laziness. Possessing seems like a lot of work. It usually means I have to leave my comfort zone, leave all that is familiar and *do* something. It means that I'll have to change and grow. Possessing most certainly means that I'll have to let go of some things in order to move on to what's been promised. I'm exhausted just thinking about possessing!

To my great relief I've discovered that laziness is not an issue unique to me. Joshua had to confront a good measure of laziness in the Israelites during his time. In fact, just before he admonished the children of Israel for not possessing what was already theirs he had a little chat with the house of Joseph to address their laziness.

In Joshua 17:14 the house of Joseph requested more land from Joshua. All the land had already been divided up but this one tribe was not satisfied. They felt they needed more land because of their size and power. Joshua agreed that they should have more land and granted them the mountains that bordered their current land. But they didn't want that land. It would take a lot of work to clear and they didn't want to work anymore. They wanted easy land, land that was move-in ready. Joshua reminded them of their own argument: they were a tribe that was great in size and power, so it should be no problem for them to clear the extra land granted to them.

It's true that stepping up and claiming the life God has for you is going to take work. You will have to let go of things, you will have to expand your capacity to live, to work, to love. You will have to push back all that doesn't belong in this new life and take the time to grow the skills and character you will need to flourish in this promised life. It's not easy and there's no quick cure for laziness. There is only the daily decision that God's promised life is worth the effort it takes to possess it.

Once you push past your fear and choose to move beyond your laziness you will probably find yourself in a moment of confusion. How exactly does one go about possessing a promise? When we are walking with God we are often required to grab hold of the intangible before we can claim the tangible. We have to trust in the unseen before we are given sight.

The writer of Hebrews explains how this works and he uses the best example possible. He references God creating the world at the beginning of time.

By faith we understand that the worlds were framed by the word of God, so that the things which are seen were not made of things which are visible. (Hebrews 11:3)

The tangible came from the intangible, the seen from the unseen. That's God's order of things. We must believe in what He says before we will see what He sees and our believing is evidenced by the words we speak. Now, I'm not talking about willy nilly name it and claim it foolishness. I'm talking about understanding God's promises and speaking those into existence into your life. I'm talking about praying scripture and setting your words to thankfulness so that your heart will follow. I'm talking about seeing things the way God sees them and not fixating on what our natural eyes can see. This is where faith steps in.

In order to possess God's promised life, you need to have faith that God will deliver. You have to put your trust in your loving heavenly Father and allow Him to guide your steps. The best way to do that is to get to know Him through His Word. Spend time reading the Bible, investigating what He has promised. Make a mess of your Bible, underline, highlight and write in the margins. Memorize the verses that speak to the promises you want to possess. Let go of your fear, laziness and confusion and step into God's promised life for you! Dive into His word and know that the trick to possessing lies in believing the unbelievable.

Chapter Thirty

BEAUTY IN BECOMING

Habakkuk 2:2&3

Then the Lord answered me and said: "Write the vision and make it plain on tablets that he may run who reads it. For the vision is yet for an appointed time; But at the end it will speak, and it will not lie. Though it tarries, wait for it; Because surely it will come, it will not tarry.

If you've made it to an age where you can read this book by yourself, you are probably carrying a little baggage from things people have said to you over time. Whether it's words of criticism or praise, those words can stay with us for a long time, especially if they are words spoken by someone whose opinion we respect and value. Words can frame your life, for better or for worse. They can build you up or box you in. Without wisdom, mentorship and Holy Spirit we can become trapped by the words spoken to us.

Although I was raised with the understanding that God created me on purpose for a purpose the whole thing seemed very vague and far off to me until I was thirteen years old. It was that fall that this far off idea suddenly became up close and personal. My pastor spoke twenty words to me, in the middle of a sermon, that have stuck with me; sometimes plaguing me, sometimes encouraging me.

It was a typical Sunday morning and I was volunteering in the two and three year-old Sunday school class. One of our little buddies was inconsolable so I was sent into the service to find his mom. As I walked along the back of the sanctuary, attempting to be as discreet as possible, my pastor spotted me from his position behind the pulpit. We made eye contact for a moment and then he continued speaking except he wasn't continuing with his sermon. He was speaking to me!

"Nicki, God wants you to know that if you follow your dreams you will be a mighty woman of God."

Then he returned to his notes and went on with his message as if nothing happened. I, on the other hand, stood rooted in my spot for several minutes, shocked, embarrassed, confused and excited. I wasn't entirely sure of what had just happened but I somehow felt marked for greatness. I eventually made my way back to the classroom and finished off the morning with those words swirling around my head and heart.

Dreams ... Mighty woman of God ... Dreams ... Mighty woman of God.

Those words have been with me from that day to this. At times they've made me feel strong and empowered, destined for some great, big, marvelous life. Other times those words have mocked me; made me feel like a ridiculous failure. I was so desperate to be something more than I was, to live up to the potential of such a declaration, that I spent years obsessively searching out my dream.

I flitted from idea to idea, with no notion of what I was really doing. My dream changed frequently and ranged from political position to social activism to hiding in mediocrity, depending on the year and my spiritual status. I had hoped that if I kept presenting God with life options He would eventually shine some kind of divine spotlight on the 'right' dream and I would finally know what would make me the mighty woman He wanted me to be. No spotlight ever shone and, in the end, all I had was a heaping pile of half-baked dreams and unrealized potential.

I wasted a lot of time chasing the wisp of something great only to end in feeling like a failure. It wasn't until I reached my thirties that I began to understand something that released me from the pressure to be great. I was finally set free to be exactly who God created me to be. I recognized that what I was lacking was the power of becoming ready in Him.

One of the incarnations of following my dream was running a very short-lived not-for-profit charity. We were a project-based organization, so depending on our resources and contacts we could be involved in anything from disaster relief, refugee care and orphan support. We had the privilege of supplying clothes and medical supplies to an orphanage in Mexico as well as the once-in-a-lifetime experience of being on the front lines of relief work after Hurricanes Katrina and Rita devastated much of the southern United States in 2005. We also got involved with a group of Congolese refugees for a period of time, assisting them to raise money to send shipments of clothes and medical supplies back to their war-torn villages.

I could write a whole book on the lessons I learned during that season of my life. It was the most frustrating, exhilarating, heart breaking and humbling misadventure I've ever experienced. God was patient and kind and gentle with me but I had a lot to learn. The first and biggest lesson I walked away from that season with was the importance of becoming ready in God.

If you become pregnant, you expect to wait at least 40 weeks for your baby to grow and develop to full health. If you want to become a doctor you expect to study and learn for years. If you want a vine-ripened tomato from your own garden you expect to do the work of planting and tending while waiting out the growing season. So if we can understand the importance of growing and learning in those scenarios why do we completely miss this concept when it comes to the things of God in our life?

It takes experience, training and growing to become who God needs us to be so we can do what He designed us to do. There are lessons to be learned and maturity to be gained as we wait for God's perfect time. When you push the dream, when you force it into existence before it's ready, before you are ready, the dream will die. I guarantee it.

It will be premature and under-developed and you will be ill equipped for the task of caring for it, nurturing it. That's what happened to me. This half-grown dream of helping people, born more from my worry that I was missing God than from my hope in Him, fought for life for a couple of years before dying in my useless arms. My desperation to do something, anything, for God caused me to force a half-grown idea into reality. That reality eventually nearly bankrupt us and disappointed the very people I meant to help. I had no idea that I had to become someone *in* Christ before I could do anything significant *for* Him.

When I began to understand the power of readiness and the beauty of becoming, my idea of significance changed completely. I gave up my pursuit of grand gestures and fame and focused on becoming more like Christ. I put all my effort into living a thankful life, an obedient life. I aspired to love more, give more and serve more. That's it. That became the dream of my heart and the measuring stick of success in my life.

I give my time, not to things that will bring me fame and popularity, but to things that will bring others into relationship with Christ. My life goal has nothing to do with personal gain and everything to do with His glory. Even in writing this book, my only focus is communicating exactly what God has put on my heart to say. No more, no less. It's up to Him who and how many read it. I do know this, though, if you are the only person meant to receive these words and this book has found its way to you then I have done something of significance for Him; I have become mighty. And I have achieved my dream in Him.

Acknowledgements

Thank you to the friends and family who contributed to this project. Thank you for believing in me, trusting me and encouraging me. You are my People and I love you!

Thank you to Pat Mohr for your guidance and assistance in getting this piece into a 'show worthy' condition. And to Joanne Hoehne and Adrienne Cornelsen, who were the first ones to 'hold my baby', thank you for being gracious, encouraging and honest … both with this book and in my life. A big thanks to my writing buddies Chris Jordan, Carolyn Burns Bass and Christine Son as well as the innumerable other writers who have influenced, instructed and inspired me with their words.

Thank you to the mighty women of faith who are mentoring me from afar. Lisa Bevere, Charlotte Gambill, Christine Caine, Priscilla Shirer, Jen Hatmaker, Bobbie Houston and Holly Wagner. We may never meet on this side of eternity but I thank you for passionately and unapologetically pursuing God's best for your life, for modeling integrity, respect and friendship and for marking the path to freedom in Christ.

Becky Nemetchek, Debbie Anderson, Todd Petkau and Craig Kennedy thank you for caring enough to speak into my life, to challenge me and to chip away at all the rough edges so more of Christ could shine through. Thank you is such an insufficient phrase when I think of my sister-friends: Sheri Martens,

Heidie Janzen, Megan Hildebrand, Mary Elias and Rachelle Dean. You have become family of my heart and my soft place to land in this town we call home. I am a better person for having your friendship!

To the other three of The Original Four. Your love, guidance and protection has been a constant in my life. Thank you for loving me and supporting me. Always.

And to my Lifetime Love and the Wee Ones ... there are no words that can ever adequately express all that is in my heart so I offer only these three ... Love you. Forever.